SMITH
SMITH
SMITH

TONY SETON KIKI

The Smiths

07 **Director's Foreword**
by Michael Rush

09 **The Smiths**
by Adrian Dannatt

21 **Tony Smith, Plates**
37 Plate List

39 **There Was a Family Named Smith**
by Gilbert Brownstone

53 **Seton Smith, Plates**
69 Plate List

71 **Seton Smith Photographs: Sensuous and Subtle Suggestions**
by David Pagel

75 **Knowing Through the Body: The Art of Kiki Smith**
by Eleanor Heartney

81 **Kiki Smith, Plates**
97 Plate List

99 **The Smiths: On the Edge of Dreams**
by Michael Rush

105 **Biographies**

Director's Foreword
by Michael Rush

It is both a pleasure and a privilege for us at the Palm Beach Institute of Contemporary Art to present this one of a kind exhibition devoted to the work of Tony, Kiki and Seton Smith. When Gilbert Brownstone first presented the idea to me not long after I arrived here, I was thrilled at the possibility. Now that it has come to pass, I am immensely grateful to Gilbert for his vision and to Kiki, Seton and the Tony Smith Estate for their steady cooperation. Sarah Auld at the Estate has been tremendously helpful since the very beginning, as has Jane Smith, wife and mother. Connecting with Jane again is a particular personal joy for me. We worked together in "downtown theater" in New York in the 1980s.

In organizing the exhibition, both Gilbert and the staff here, especially our Curatorial Coordinator, Jody Servon, have made no attempt to force similarities among the artists. That each is an extraordinary artist is already clear and well known. They are also part of the same family, which, as those of us who come from families of one kind or another (and that would be all of us) know well is a combination of all manner of facts, emotions, dispositions and mysteries. This exhibition wisely spares the living and the dead any psychologizing or aesthetic speculations. This is not to say that the catalogue writers have not permitted themselves certain musings about the Smiths. And why not? Hopefully, one of the contributions of the exhibition and the thought that has gone into it will be to open a door toward future scholarship about this family of artists.

I want to extend thanks to all who have made so many essential contributions to this exhibition. In addition to Gilbert, Kiki, Seton, Jane and Sarah I thank Jody who has overseen all aspects of the exhibition, including the catalogue. Thanks and congratulations to Cornelia Blatter and Marcel Hermans at COMA for their exquisite catalogue which also contains the enduringly valuable contributions of my writer colleagues Eleanor Heartney, Adrian Dannatt and David Pagel.

Our staff has also contributed greatly to the many efforts involved in the exhibition. Thanks especially to Phillip Estlund, our Registrar and Kurt Bretz our Chief Preparator and their crew for their customary excellence. I thank Anne Edgar, NY, for her superior Public Relations management of this exhibition. Special thanks to Paula Matthews, our Office Manager, Kara Walker-Tomé, our Education Director, as well as Sybillé Canthal and Haley Shaw for their curatorial assistance.

We are very grateful for the generosity and cooperation of galleries, lenders and benefactors. I want to thank Mitchell-Innes and Nash Gallery, PaceWildenstein Gallery, Winston Wächter Mayer Fine Art, and Matthew Marks Gallery in New York, Barbara Krakow Gallery in Boston and Galerie Cent 8 in Paris. Special thanks to Emily Fisher Landau.

All the programs of PBICA are supported through the extraordinary generosity of our founders, Robert and Mary Montgomery. They are responsible for our "family" here at PBICA and it is thanks to their unique vision for the importance of contemporary art in our community that we are able to celebrate the Smith "family" in this very special way.

The Smiths

by Adrian Dannatt

It's noble to refuse to be added up or divided.
- Frank O'Hara

Obviously, the tradition of the artist-family is as long as the history of art itself, and, as most artists were male, that lineage was also inherently masculine, a paternal apprenticeship appropriate to the trade's artisan origins. This custom has always been accompanied by a corollary debate as to the, literally, "relative" merits of one artist and the other, the ranking and rating of father versus son, brother versus sibling. It is equally part of this tradition to claim that, in fact, these artists have really *nothing* in common other than being of the same family, that there is no valid point of comparison beyond shared nomenclature. This is as true of the Smith family as it was of, say, Tiepolo; the natural human fascination with family dynamics is offset by stern claims that all such anecdotage is irrelevant to any serious judgment of the work. Both of these views are equally honest and, like many mutually exclusive positions, are best enjoyed when paradoxically conjoined. As much academic ink has been devoted to the vast differences between the paintings of Tiepolo father and son as to the contrary argument that their styles are almost indistinguishable. These opinions live through and within each other, depend upon the other, agree to disagree—as indeed family members do, irreconcilable and co-dependent.

It would be fair to say that there is clearly no point of correspondence between the oeuvre of Tony Smith and that of his daughters Kiki and Seton. Any attempt to create links between such disparate works would surely be doomed to tenuous analogy or oblique waffle. Forcing together three deliberately different aesthetics just for the sake of pleasing familial symmetry recalls T.S. Eliot's description of Donne as "yoking together" disparate elements by metaphor alone. But just as the entire premise of a "yoked" triptych of Smith talents could be dismissed as gimmick, it also makes an immediately engaging theme. As a fascinating exercise in contrasts, which simultaneously sharpens one's appreciation of each artist, such a grouping serves less as a study of the Smiths per se than as an essay on all the varied ways of art-making in the late 20th century.

To bring together three overtly different aesthetics on the basis of name alone is a positively diacritical exercise in comparative analysis. A shared name, or even just shared initials, seems as fruitful a method of arranging a group show as any other. Indeed, the first show of the Society of Independent Artists in 1917 was installed, at Duchamp's suggestion, by chance drawing of alphabetical letters from a hat. Jacques Derrida, a master of the "improper" use of proper names, exploits family titles such as Ponge for puns, games and fertile word-play that expand the intellectual territory. Through anagram, etymology or other diacritical features, a proper name can link itself to a range of very different concepts, images or objects. Such proper-name associations, a series of linked puns, could equally be used to bring different artists into contact—just as acceptable a basis for their inclusion in an exhibition as any other, in fact more rigorous because so predetermined. A whole show devoted to the work of all artists who happen to be called Stella, or a museum grouping of every single artist named Smith who ever lived would doubtless prove as fertile in works and rewards as an exhibition of only those directly related. Language and its manifold layered reverberations may be as good a curatorial strategy as visual analogy.

Of course, issues of envy, jealousy, competition and career-anxiety are excluded from professional art criticism to the same degree that they are vitally, painfully present in the everyday life of every artist of every epoch. Such topics are utterly verboten within academic art history, even though they remain the dominant constants within the art world at any time or place. Likewise, most artists and art-related individuals cannot resist rating and ranking their immediate contemporaries, a hugely enjoyable game of fixing a hierarchy of talent. Earlier art historians also enjoyed this sport, or a more elegant and measured version of it; ordering a strict list of "best" artists was considered central to their work as judges. In contemporary criticism, such football tables are ruled demodé and bad form; indeed, making any value judgment seems suspicious. All this is further compounded if those being compared are father-and-daughter as opposed to father-and-son. During the recent American exhibition on the Gentileschi family, the most famous example of father-daughter artists, most agreed that Artemesia was star of the show, even if it was also admitted that her father was probably, technically, the better artist. Issues of sexism, censorship, patriarchal condescension or even brute physical factors—rape in Artemesia's case—make judging female artists a rather more delicate task.

Despite all this, there exist pleasing examples of female painters who have entirely eclipsed the careers of their artist fathers, truly "taken" their names. Angelica Kaufmann's father was a minor ecclesiastical muralist who gave up making art to manage his daughter's business affairs, and Elizabeth Vigèe-Lebrun's pater was a pastel portraitist of whom almost nothing is known. The great fame, contemporary and current, of both these painters left their fathers' work entirely forgotten, a classic family dynamic. The legend of Rosa Bonheur, a cross-dressing adventurer who dissected beast parts and roamed the slaughterhouses of Paris, exists in a vacuum despite a household of artist siblings and her father's once-fabled animal paintings. Nor does the career of Frida Kahlo, most celebrated female artist of the last century, depend much on the oeuvre of her obscure father, an exiled German photographer, though both created striking self-portraits. There are also a few, far-rarer cases of well-respected artist mothers and their equally talented offspring, such as Suzanne Valadon and her illegitimate son, Maurice Utrillo.

Because of the nature of family life and the professional structure of painting as a craft, there are far more examples of father-daughter artist duos in the centuries preceding the 20th. The invention of modernism and "originality" meant that practical skills of art-making were less likely to be passed down between generations than those of carpenters or vintners. In a family where the father was a professional artist and had no son to inherit his business, it was normal that the daughter, educated at home, could take this role. Thus from the 16th century onwards we have a surprisingly long litany of father-daughter names, including Prospero and Lavinia Fontana, Jan and Clara Peeters or Nunzio Galizia and his daughter Fede, who had already become a renowned portraitist by the time she was twelve. This lineage continued throughout the 19th century, for as long as art was still a regulated profession, exemplified by Marie Eleanor Godefroid (1778-1849), whose father had lodgings in the Louvre, or by Sarah Miriam Peale (1800-1885), a well-known portraitist and part of the fabled Peale family. Nor are artist-sisters unknown to history, the classic example being Sofonisba Anguissola, the first famed female artist, born in 1532, and her sister Lucia

Anguissola (1540-1565), who, if she had lived longer, would probably have surpassed her older sister in talent and renown. This historical aside, mentioned in all accounts of the two sisters, is typical of the slightly snide, competitive tone sibling artists seem to engender.

More typical of this sordid territory is the rivalry between brother and sister artists, especially when the emphasis shifted to unique genius rather than hereditary ability. The life of Gwen John was dominated and shaped to every degree by the vast success of her brother Augustus; her paintings and her small career were essentially a negative space carved out of her brother's fame as Britain's greatest artist. Nobody could have imagined how the reputation of Augustus would dwindle while Gwen has become locus of widespread appreciation and fascination. The two careers reversed each other with a neat exactitude no fairy tale could match, but, just as when they were alive, their current status is entirely symbiotic, linked eternally. An equally extreme, more recent example of brother-sister rivalry is provided by acclaimed Australian artist Mike Parr, whose sister Julie, a feminist artist also based in Sydney, has reversed her family name to Rrap. This meta-linguistic-protest against her brother's presumed dominance is a direct blow against the name itself and the name's embodied patriarchal system, nothing less than Jacques Lacan's "Name-of-the Father."

These two daughters of Tony share a generic Name-of-the-Father *par excellence*, the least remarkable, most common surname, that of Smith. Indeed, the name Smith is so neutral and ubiquitous one can vanish into it. Yet the first name of each daughter is both dramatic and unusual, especially in the context of America at the time they were named: Chiara, born in 1954, and Seton and her twin sister Beatrice, the next

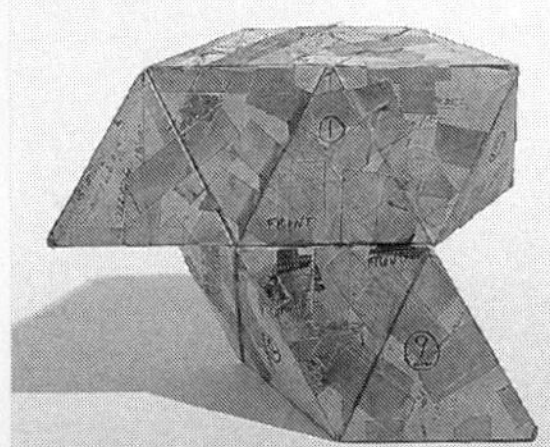

TONY SMITH
TAU, 1961-62

year. The flat gender-ambiguity of the name Seton is contrasted to the notable femininity of the Italianate Chiara. Neither of these daughters changed her family name, but Chiara became Kiki, linked irresistibly to that other Kiki, she of Montparnasse, embodiment of Parisian bohemia while also a strong survivor and charming artist in her own right. In French *kiki* is also a term for the gullet and throat, body parts surely appropriate to Kiki Smith's sculpture. More remarkably, in France, where Seton has lived and worked for long periods, *séton* is a medieval term for an arcane catheter made from catgut passed beneath the skin, the extremities exiting from two different orifices to assure continuous drainage. "*Je suis encore au lit, avec un séton dans le cou*" ("I am still in bed, with a tube in the neck") as Flaubert put it. Equally, a *séton* can describe the entry and exit points, the cutaneous orifices, of a wound made by a projectile passing through soft body tissue. Such images clearly conjure Kiki's work in themselves, her bodily aesthetic oddly embodied in the Name-of-the-Sister.

Of course the Lacanian schema of the Name-of-the-Father is inherently linked to the accompanying Death-of-the-Father, the continuation of the dead patriarchal model by language alone, by immortal lineage of naming. Within this context it seems normal that both Kiki and Seton should have begun their careers in 1980 with the *Times Square Show*, the first time they exhibited their work together. Not only were they young, 25 and 24, but also that was the year their father died. By the time of his demise, Tony Smith had become a "famous" artist. While his daughters had worked with him in creating some of his structures, notably *Bat Cave* of 1969, his relative celebrity and success ensured that as independent artists, neither daughter wished to make work similar to his. Actually, as an artist who stressed the physical, technical

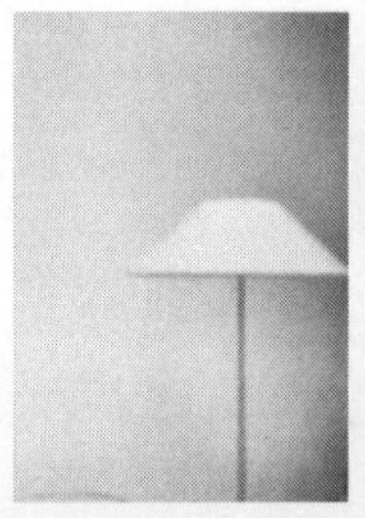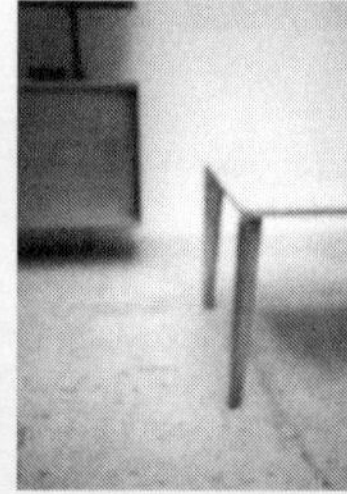

SETON SMITH
CHEZ P.S., 2000

craftsmanship behind his work, Tony could well have apprenticed his daughters to the workshop in the old way. As it was, both Kiki and Seton produced work that is deliberate antithesis of their father's aesthetic, an extreme contrast almost comic in its militancy. Both daughters use shades of abstraction, as color and camouflage, but the monumental abstract is so associated with Tony's work that it is forbidden territory—not because they would be accused of being derivative or unimaginative but rather to leave his legacy, his own field of command untouched, clean of any incestuous "anxiety of influence" even in retrospect.

To set Seton Smith's images of lush, elegant interiors against the rigorous modernist architecture designed by her father is to witness a "return of the real," the excluded elements of Tony's aesthetic being acknowledged, allowed back. Everything carefully removed from the world by Tony, all the clutter of soi-disant elegance, the chandeliers, the pouffes, the gilt and decorative curlicues, floods back. In Seton's series entitled *Chez P.S.*, images of what looks like furniture by Jean Prouvé or Royère, we sense an homage to the modern style of her upbringing, to Tony Smith's own deep love of good design. But this autobiographical nod is kept discrete, blurred by a distance of both time and attitude, a certain *froideur* that keeps sentiment at bay. Tony created buildings as an architect and his larger sculptures serve as buildings in themselves, as anyone who has sheltered from the rain under the lip of *Tau* outside Hunter College will gratefully attest. The solid metal mass of such sculptures, the limited palette of black or dark blue and the angularity of each element provide vivid antitheses to the salons and embassies Seton captures in edible tones. Her work may be soaked in rich color, sensual associations and an almost subaqueous nostalgia,

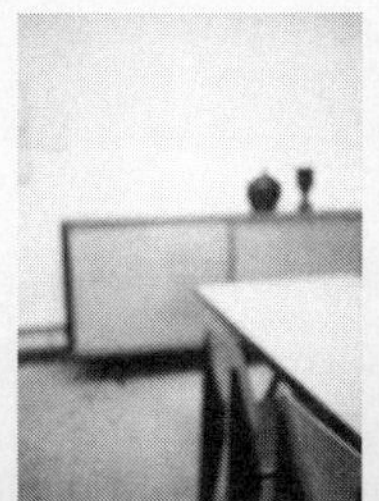
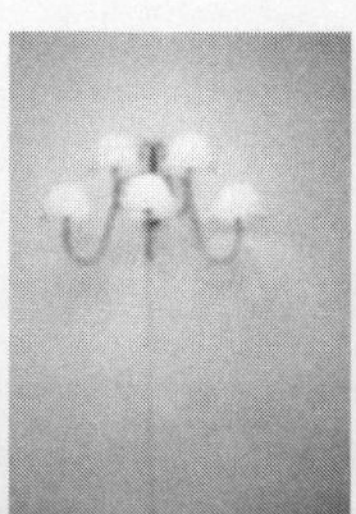
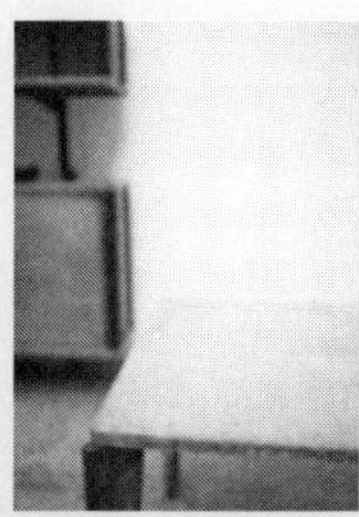

SETON SMITH
CHEZ P.S., 2000

but the intellectual clarity behind these images is as sharp as their focus is soft. This radical shift between the "hardness" and "sharpness" of Tony's work and the softness and fog (a French term, *flou*, has the onomatopoeic advantage) of Seton's imagery could not be more deliberate. Likewise, the tactile delicacy and fragility of Kiki's oeuvre positions itself with reference to the abstract "brutality" of her father's work, his mammoth metal cube versus her tissue-paper tracings as cartoon opponents. None of this contrast should be reduced to gender essentialism that reads Tony's work as inherently male and his daughter's as equally female. Tony was certainly the least "macho" and most cultivated of men, an expert on poetry, ballet, literature and mysticism. His creative work came out of an intellectual and sensual logic very far from the heroic physicality of the typical minimal or Abstract Expressionist practitioner. He was anything but a boor.

Disregarding the whole moot issue of female/delicate and male/strong, which could easily, too easily, determine a casual glance at the varied works of the Smith family, it is, however, clear that the art produced by the sisters is blatantly, self-consciously "Other" to the weighty "Real" of the father. One might even nurture a fantasy that both Kiki and Seton have tucked away in the very back of their studios some fifteen-foot welded-bronze behemoth with jet-black patina, that both of them at least tried to make one of these things during their early careers, gave it a go, got it out of their system, and then began to make art as absolutely different as it could be. Indeed, the maturing sophistication of Kiki's and Seton's work can be judged by the degree to which they are prepared to sail closer and closer to potential comparison with the work of their father. Previously they seemed to be avoiding his legacy at all costs, even

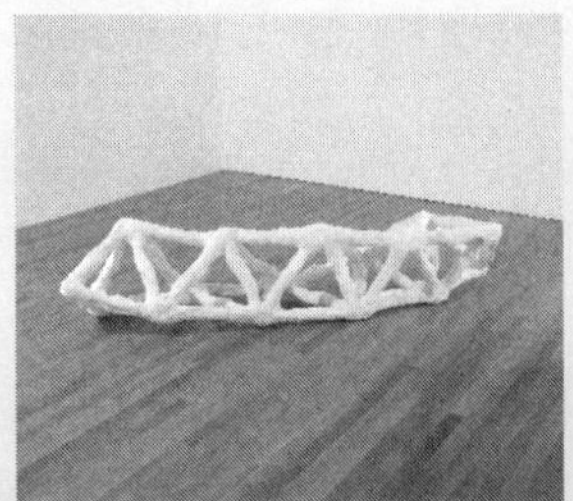
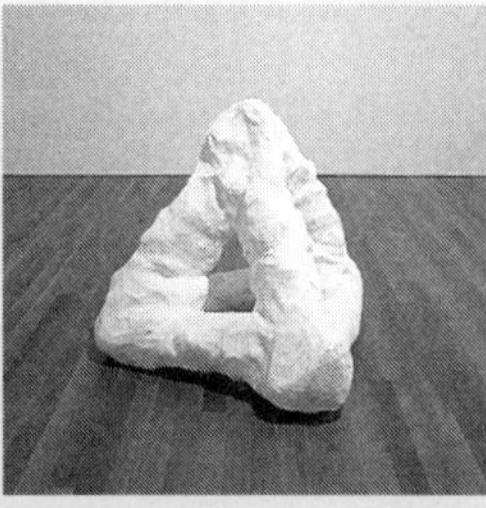

TONY SMITH
LEFT, *WINGBONE*, 1962
RIGHT, *TETRAHEDRON*, 1961

at the expense of not doing what they would like to for fear of any faint correspondence. Similarly, in the case of another modern abstract master, Kenneth Noland and
his daughter Cady, the vast difference between their work, the impossible distance
between materials and styles, has gradually diminished. Eventually Cady could make
paintings indistinguishable from Noland Senior and they would have to be considered
not as capitulation but confidence.

And of course, on extremely close scrutiny, there are points of resemblance in
the art of Tony Smith and his daughters. Examining even a single example of his large
sculptures, one realizes how many flaws and nicks, chips and scratches time or van-
dalism has inflicted upon their theoretically perfect surfaces. There is a whole micro-
narrative, a puzzle of details, to be closely read on these far-from-flawless planes, a
very human intimacy in the grain itself. Kiki uses individual parts to assemble a sculptural whole, like her father, and also tends to work in her living room rather than in a
studio, a domestic touch adopted from him. The paper and cardboard and plaster Tony
used to build his maquettes are all materials very dear to his daughter. One only has
to look at his white plaster sculptures, such as 1962's *Wingbone* (a very Kiki Smith
title for a piece that actually belongs to her) or *Tetrahedron* of 1961, to see obvious
points of confluence between father and daughter. Likewise, Tony's cardboard models
for *She Who Must Be Obeyed, Yellowbird* or *Tau* share elements with Kiki's work, albeit
by accidents of discoloration and wear. More obviously, his 1937-38 sketchbooks of
individual cells or his 1943 drawings of male and female genitals could almost be
confused with Kiki's work. Equally, if one wanted to push such preposterous analogies
(for what do they actually prove, that these artists really were the children of their

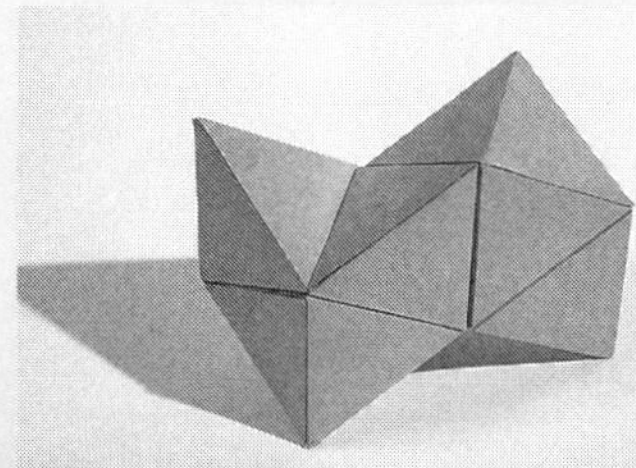

TONY SMITH
YELLOWBIRD, 1971

father?), one could draw a parallel between Tony's vaporous and cloudy oil paintings of 1956 (pp 118-119 in MOMA catalogue) and the dissolving tableaux of Seton.

Lacan explains that logically Woman is one of the Names-of-the-Father, that the signifier for Woman may occupy the place of the father—exception to the rule of castration—because she is as uncastrated as he is. It is better the father remains uncastratable above all else, better murdered, better dead. It would be facile to read Tony's sculpture as literally "phallic" and thus assume that, having taken the "Name-of-the-Father," Kiki and Seton have symbolically castrated his phallic potency, his absent role as master. Tony, with his beard, racing cars and erect forms, could easily act the phallic (paternal) signifier within this symbolic order and play the role with comic relish as a well-read Freudian. But then we would be obliged to assign roles of the "hysteric," the "obsessive" and the "neurotic" within this tight familial field, to carry through to the bitter end such inherently unrewarding analysis. For in this case, behind the metaphor of the paternal symbol is the actual father himself. The father is not a signifier, it's a name, and its place has to be absolutely void and kept as a void. But as Lacan said of Freud, he was not only dead physically, he also played the part of the dead father for the international analytic movement, thus sustaining it. Similarly, the oeuvre of Tony Smith is sustained by the extreme "difference" of his daughters' art, by mutual refusal to accept any comparisons as may be here offered.

Adrian Dannatt is a poet and New York correspondent for *The Art Newspaper* and *Flash Art*.

SMITH
TONY
SMITH

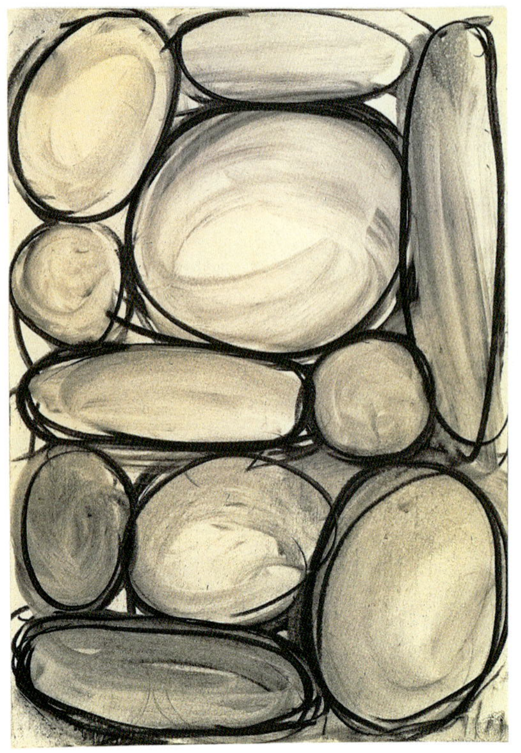 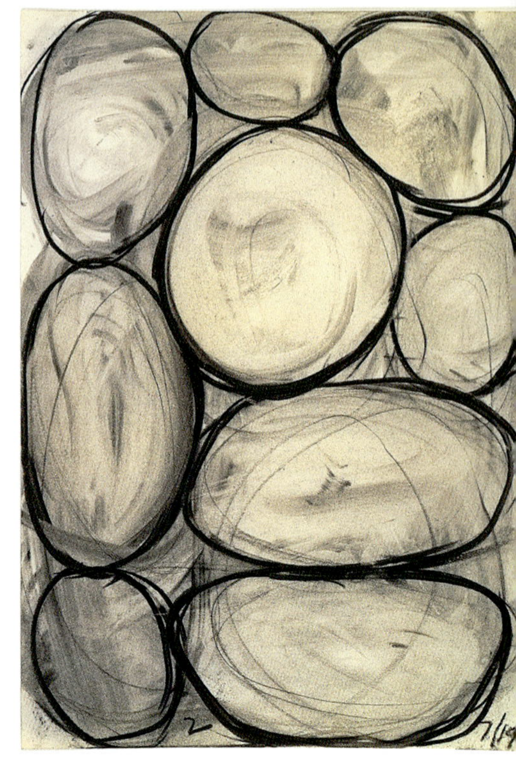

22/23

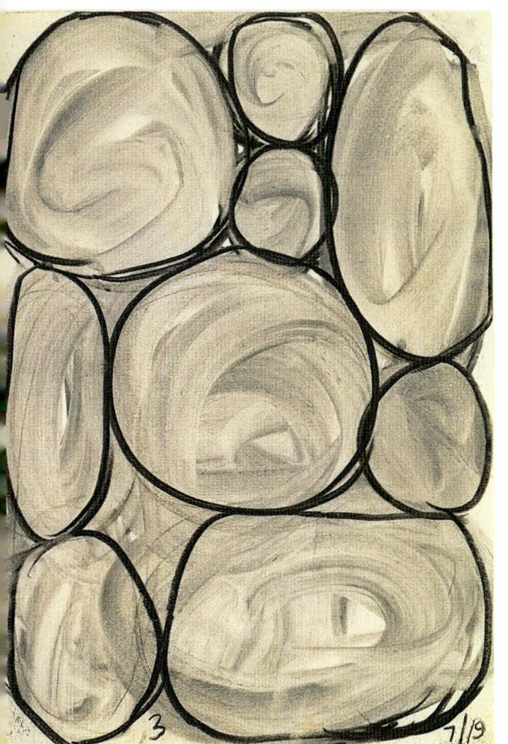
3
7/19

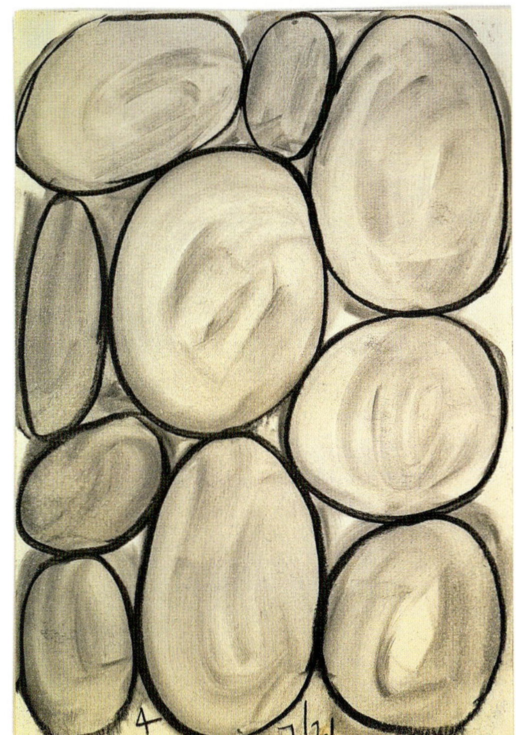
4
7/21

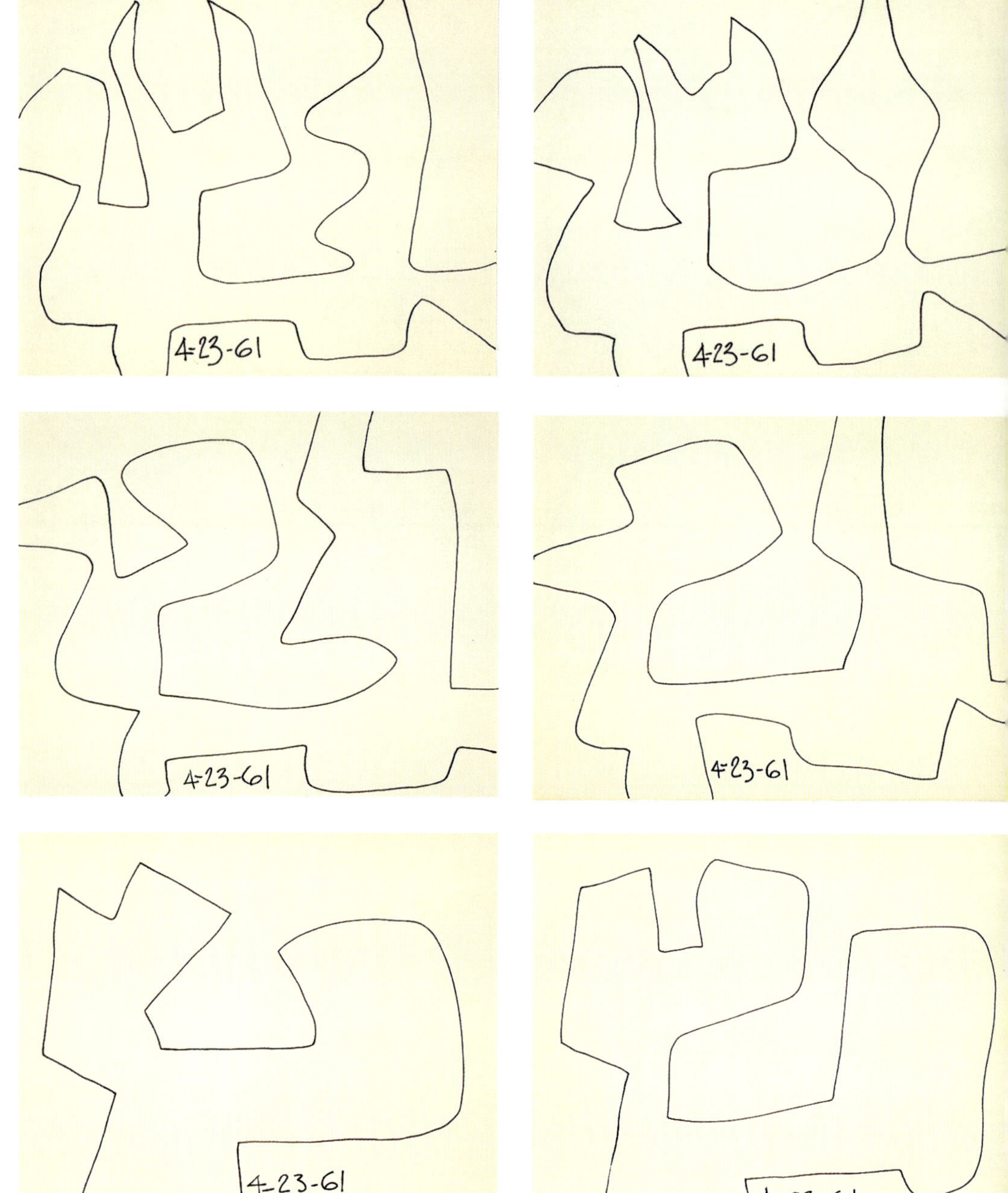

4-23-61
4-23-61
4-23-61
4-23-61
4-23-61
4-23-61

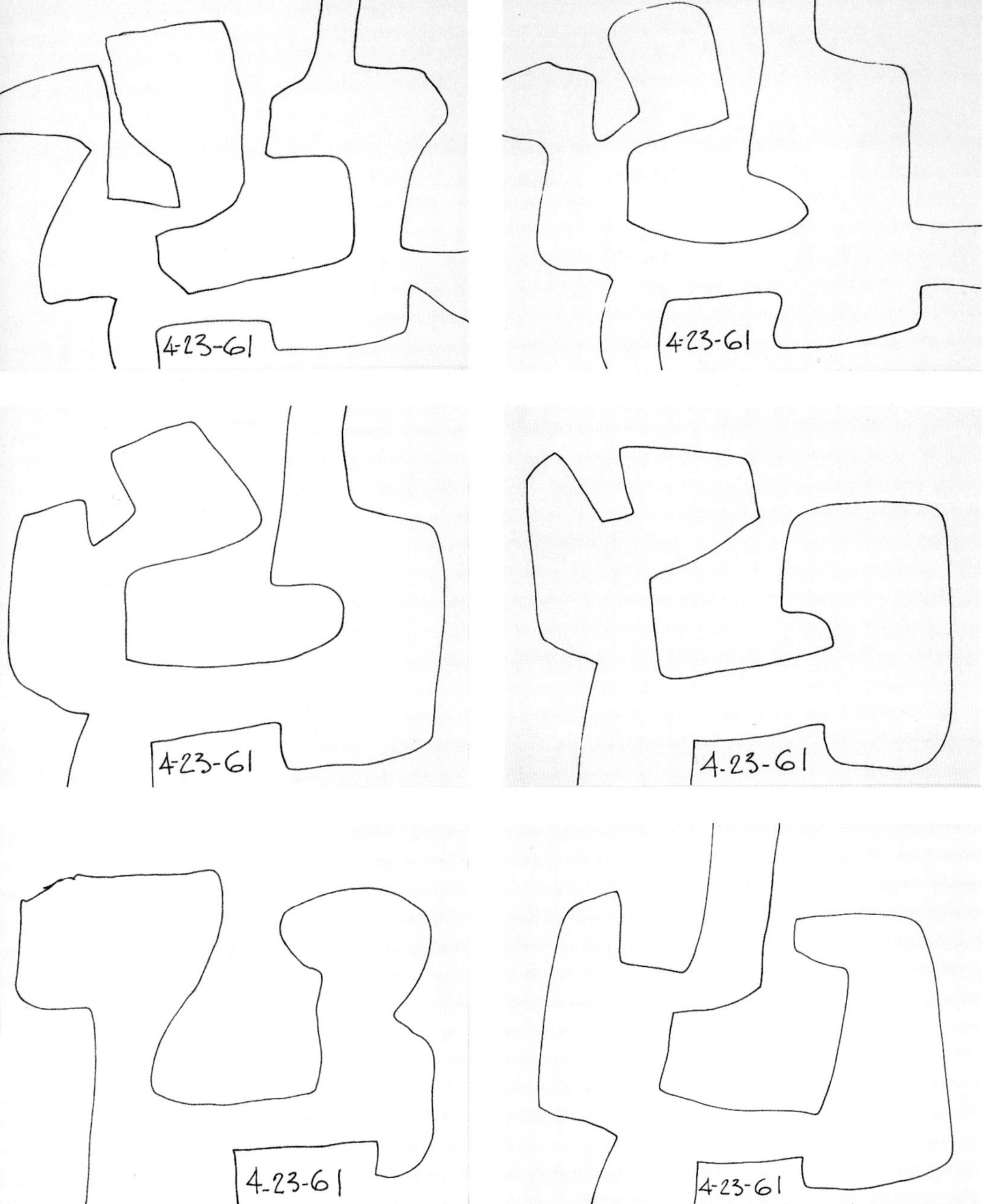

4-23-61
4-23-61
4-23-61
4.23-61
4-23-61
4-23-61

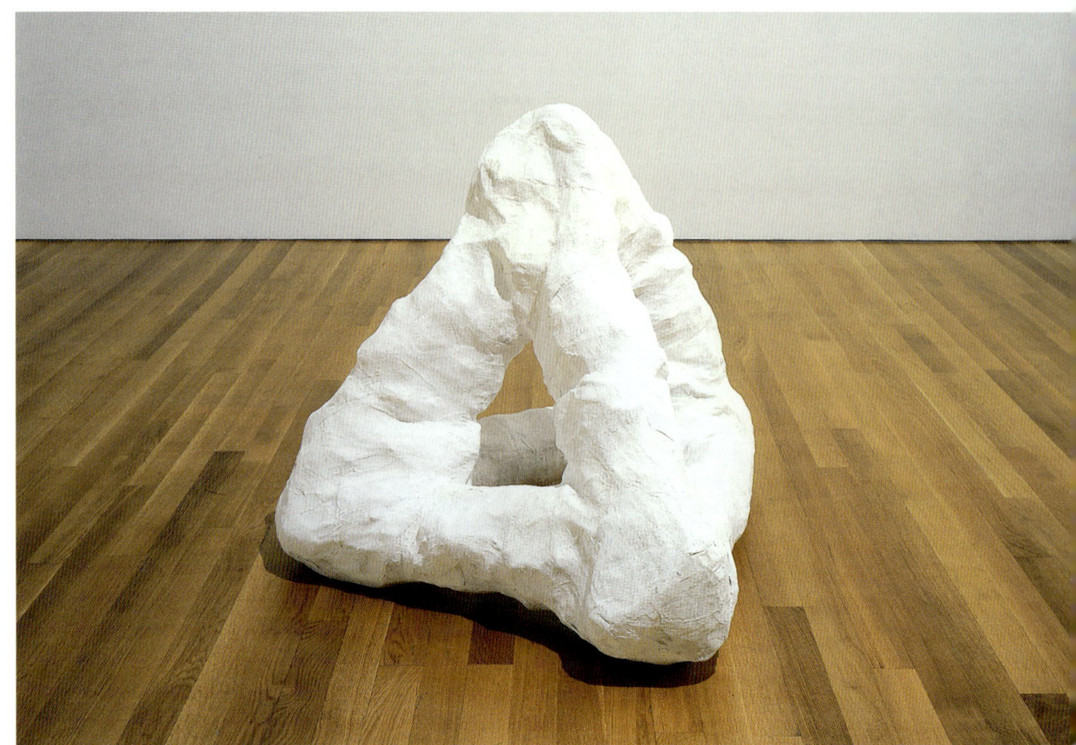

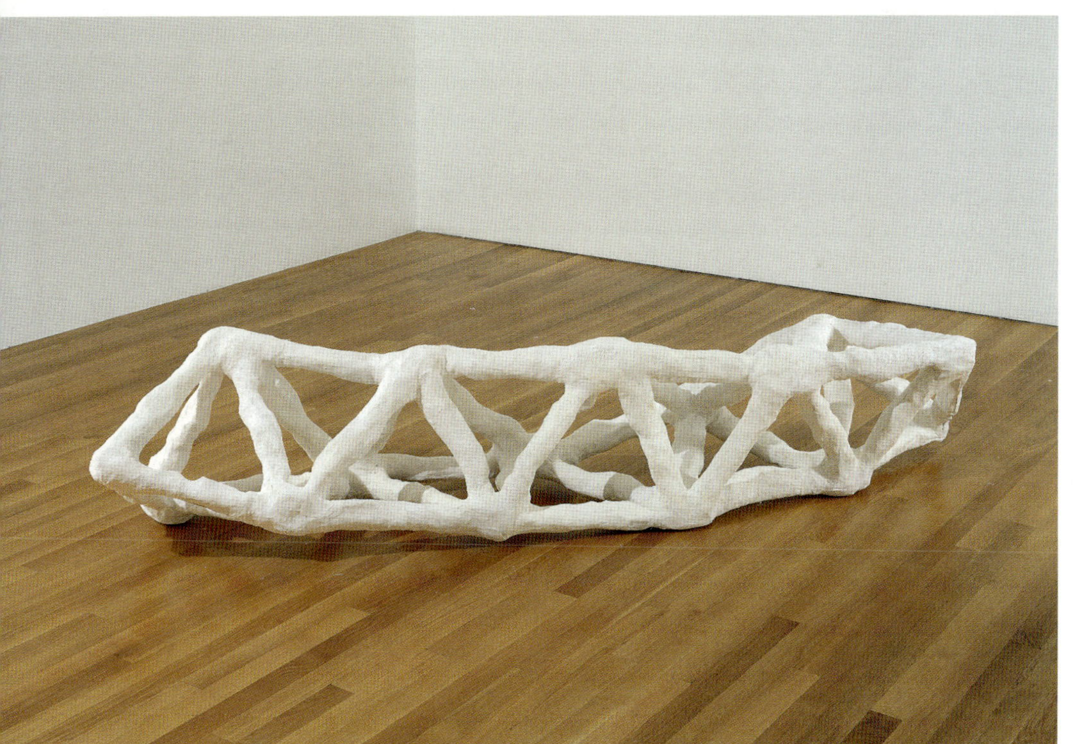

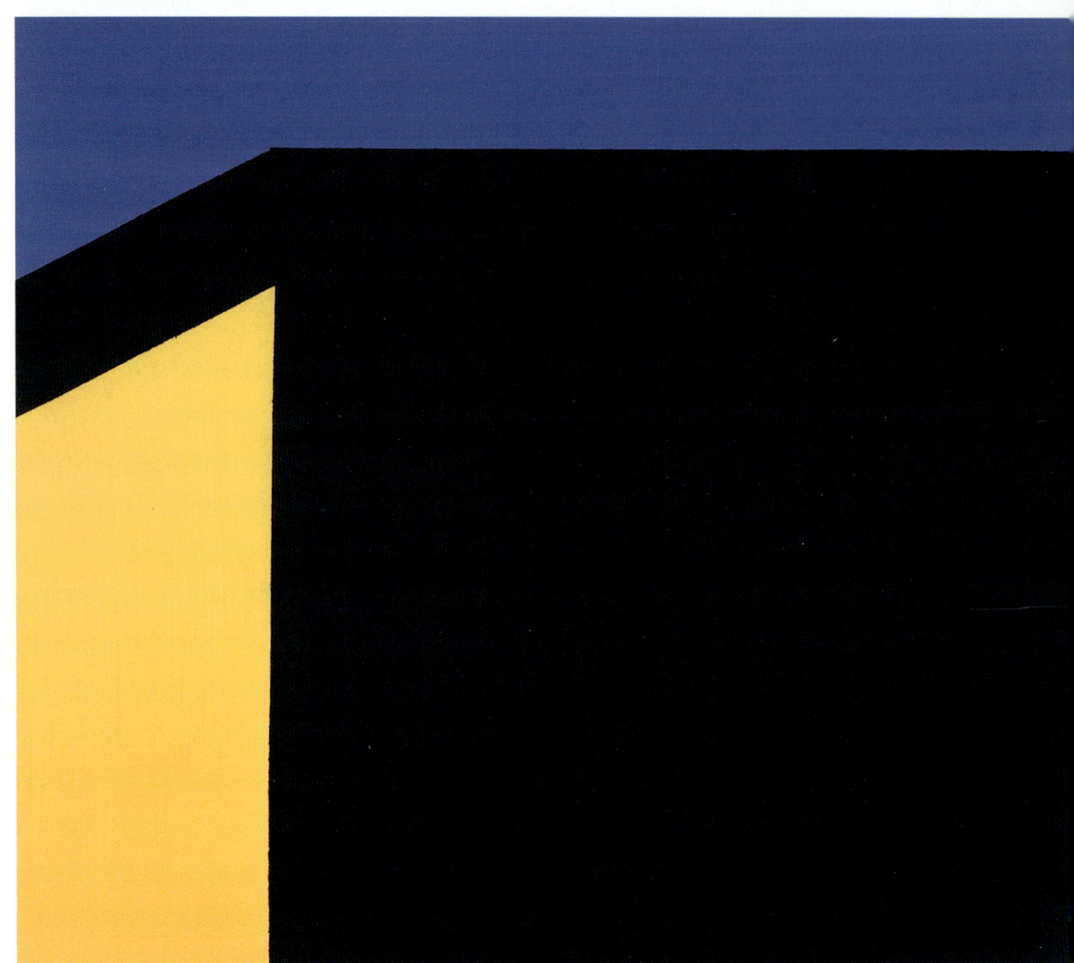

28/29

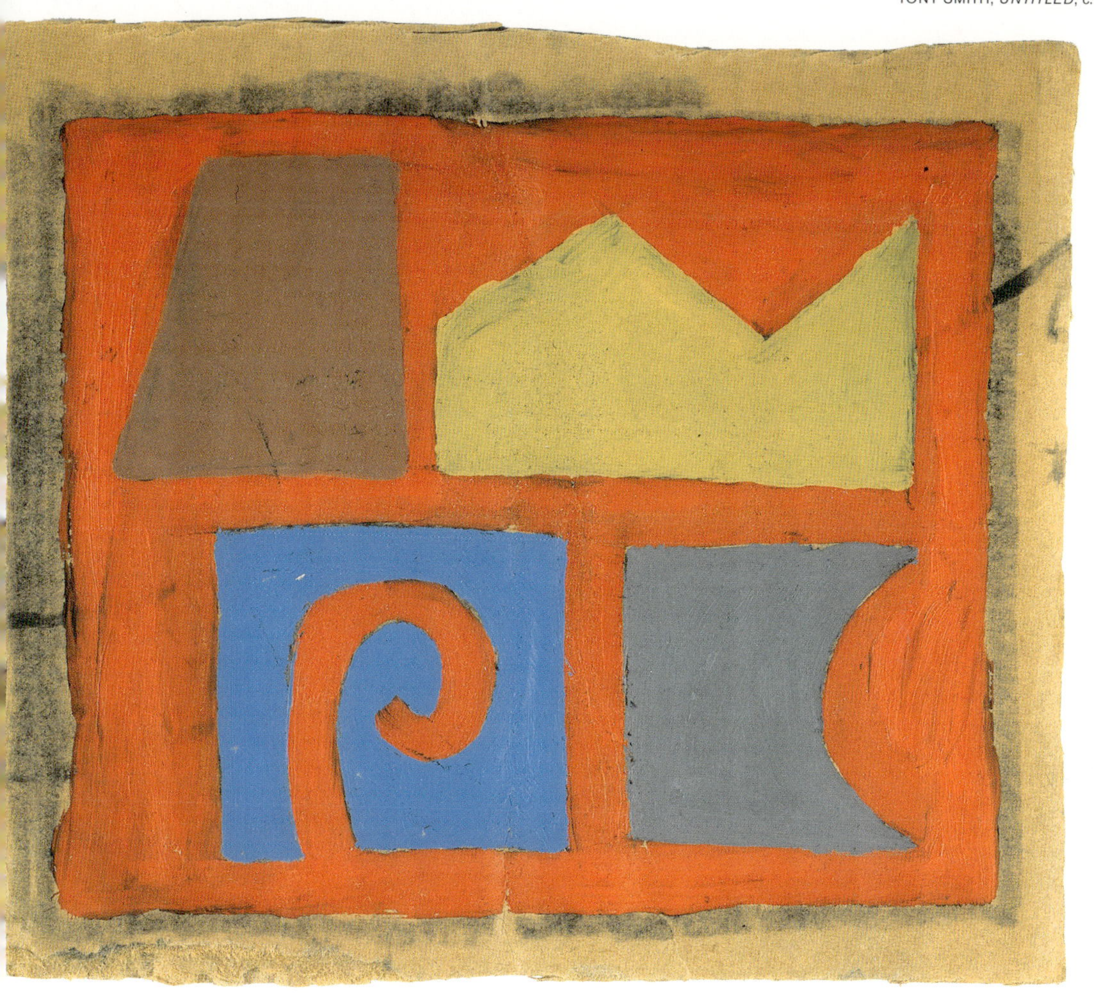

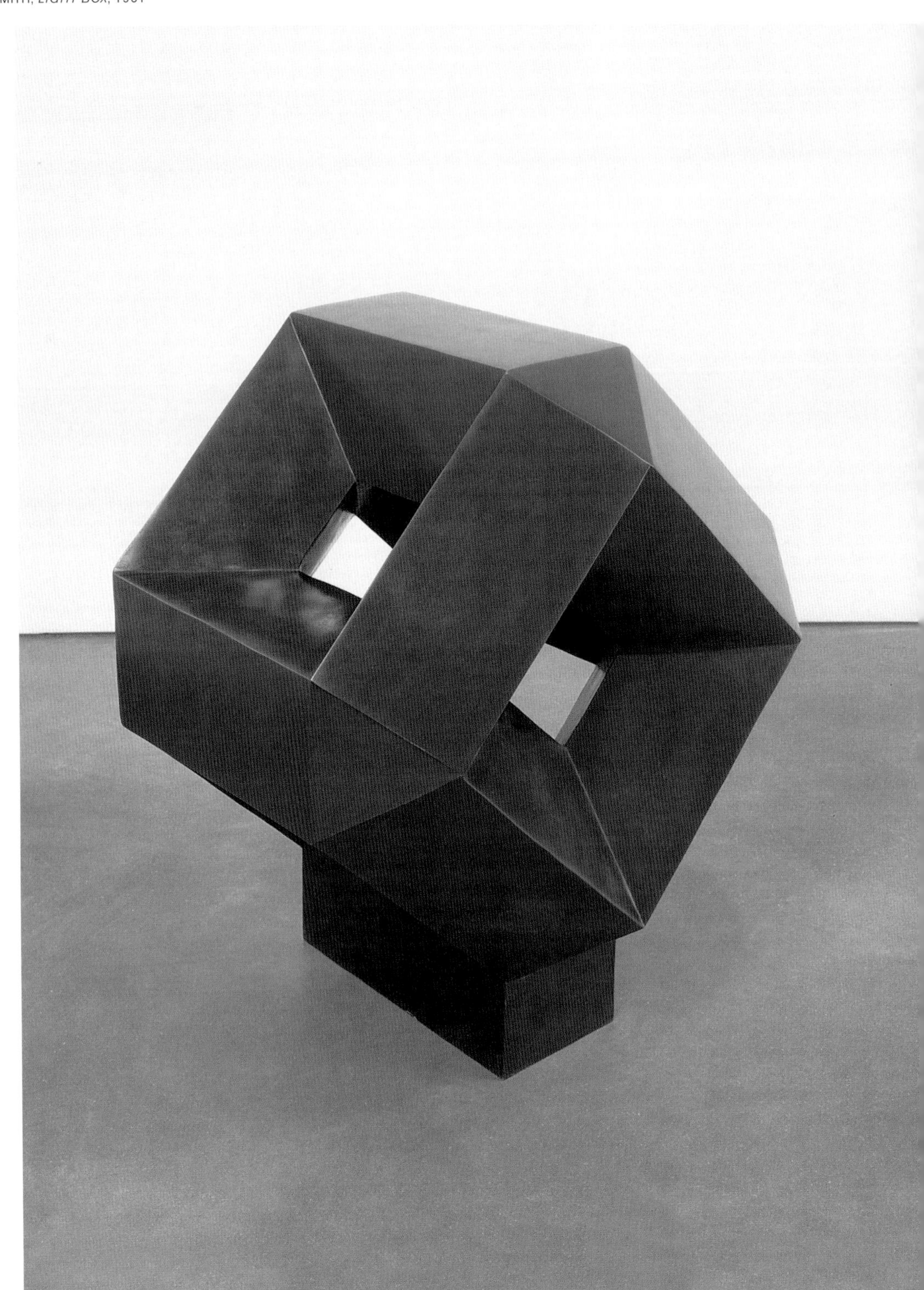

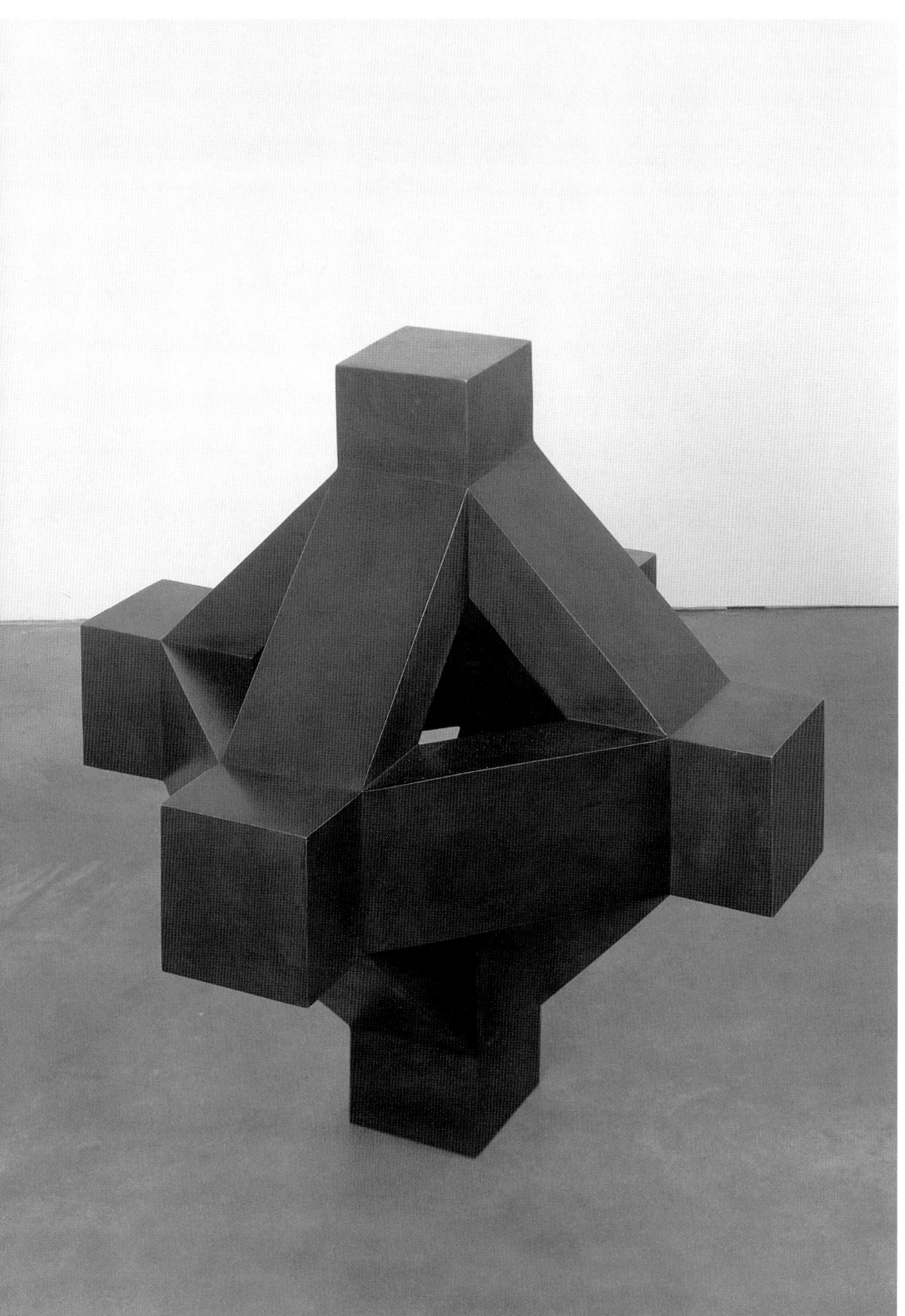

TONY SMITH, *CROSS*, 1960-62

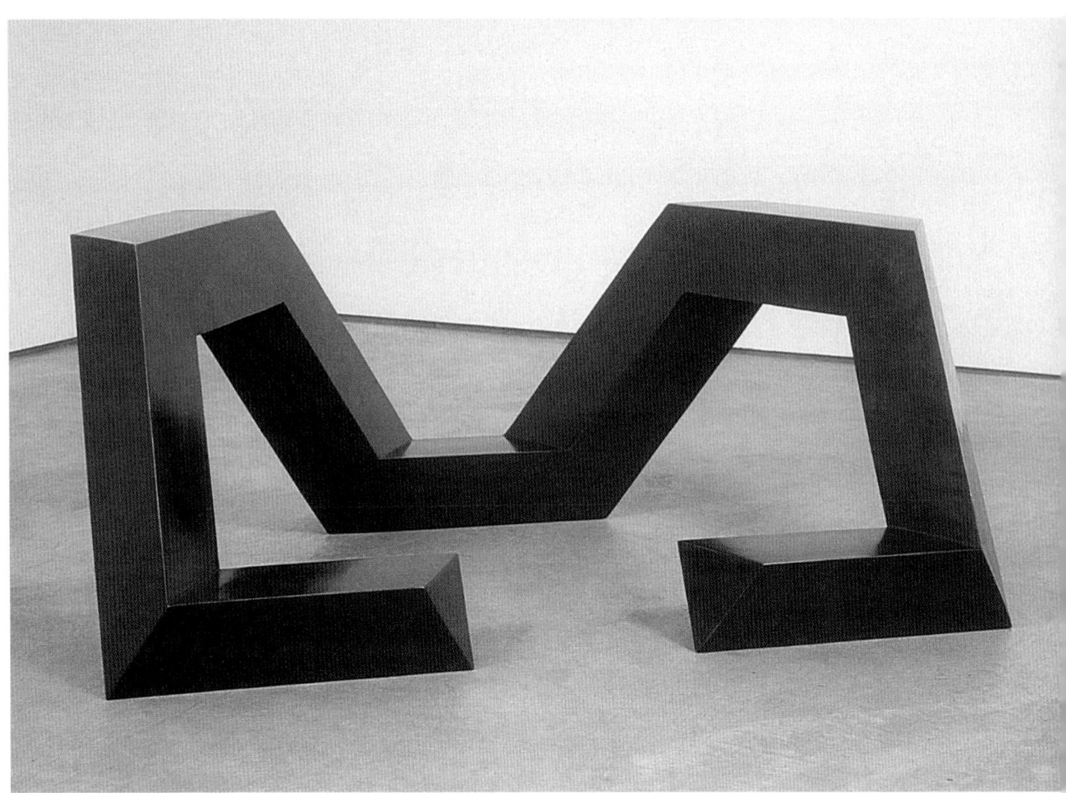

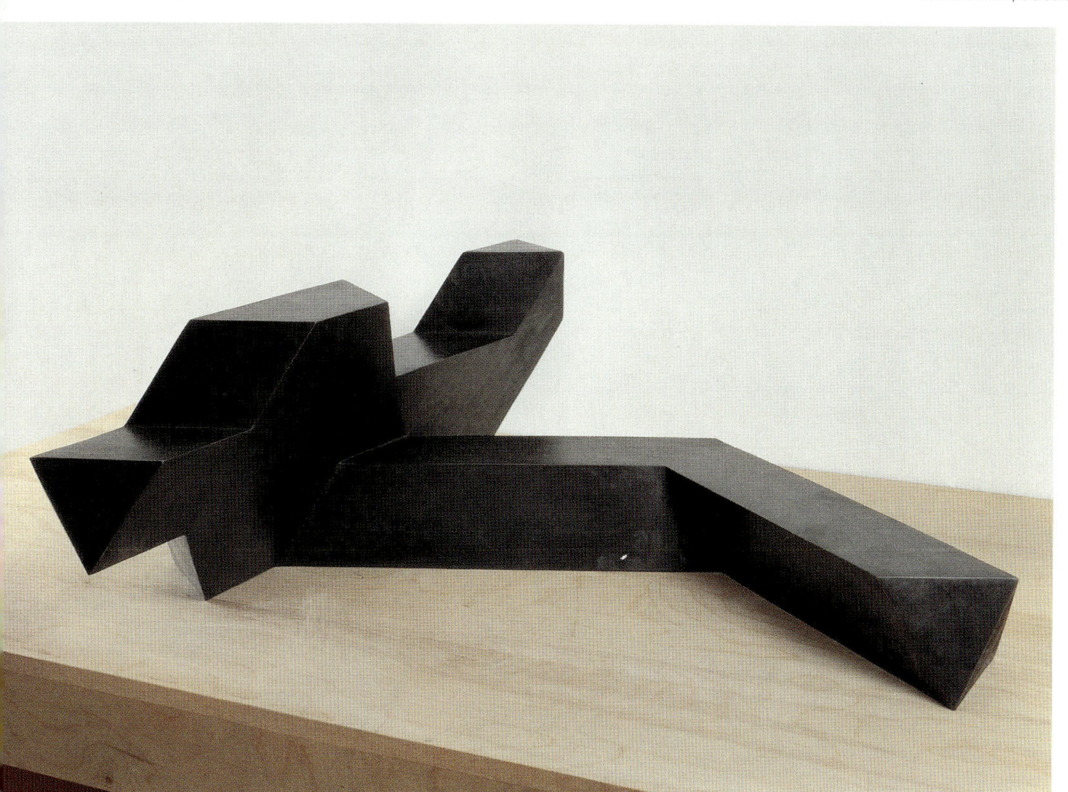

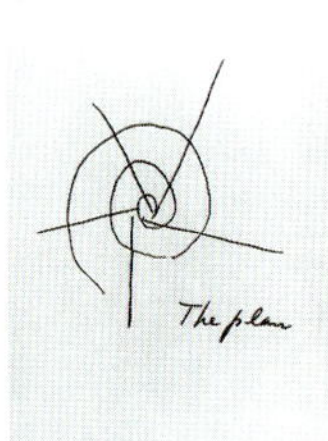

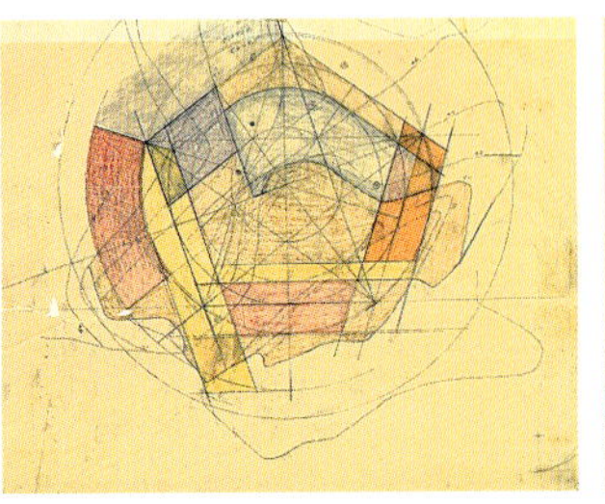

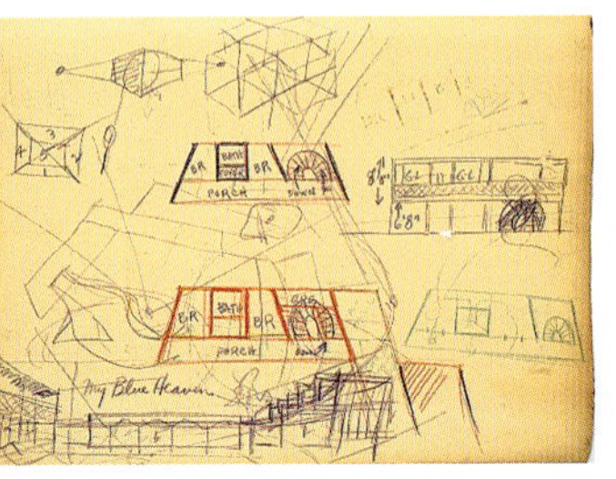

34/35

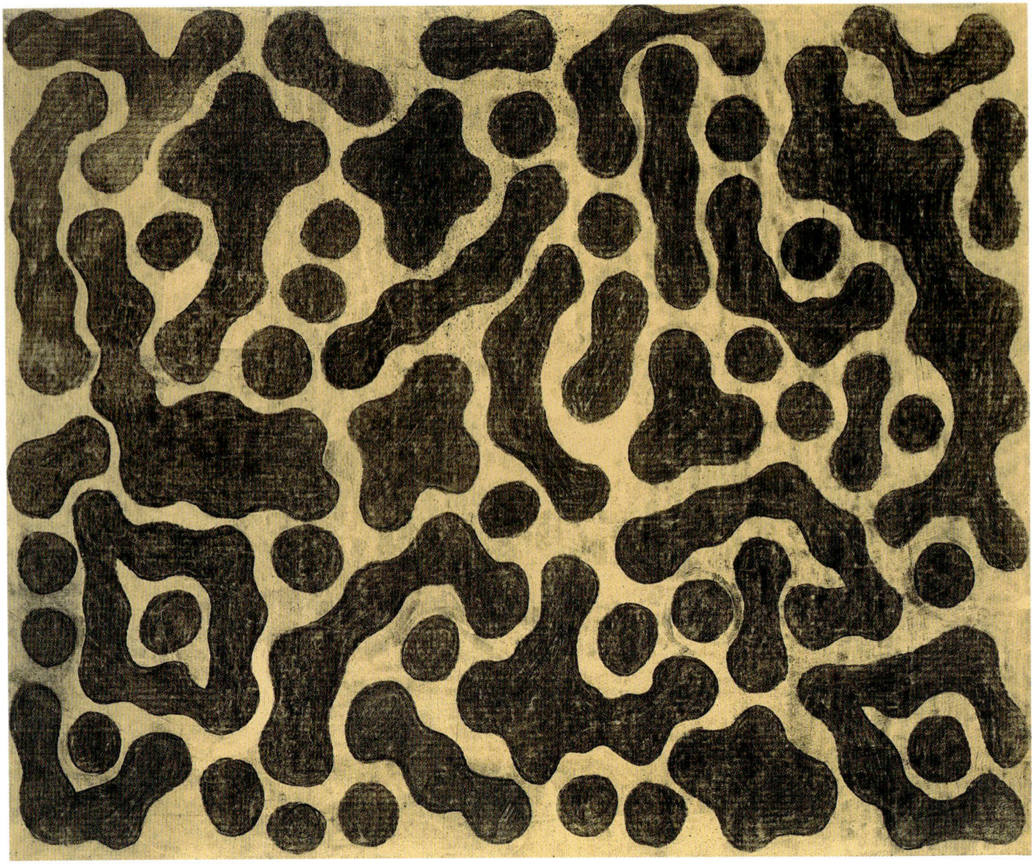

TONY SMITH
LEFT, PAGE FROM A
SKETCHBOOK c.1945
CENTER, *OLSEN HOUSE*
(PLAN) c.1951
RIGHT, *MY BLUE HEAVEN*
(OLSEN HOUSE) c.1951

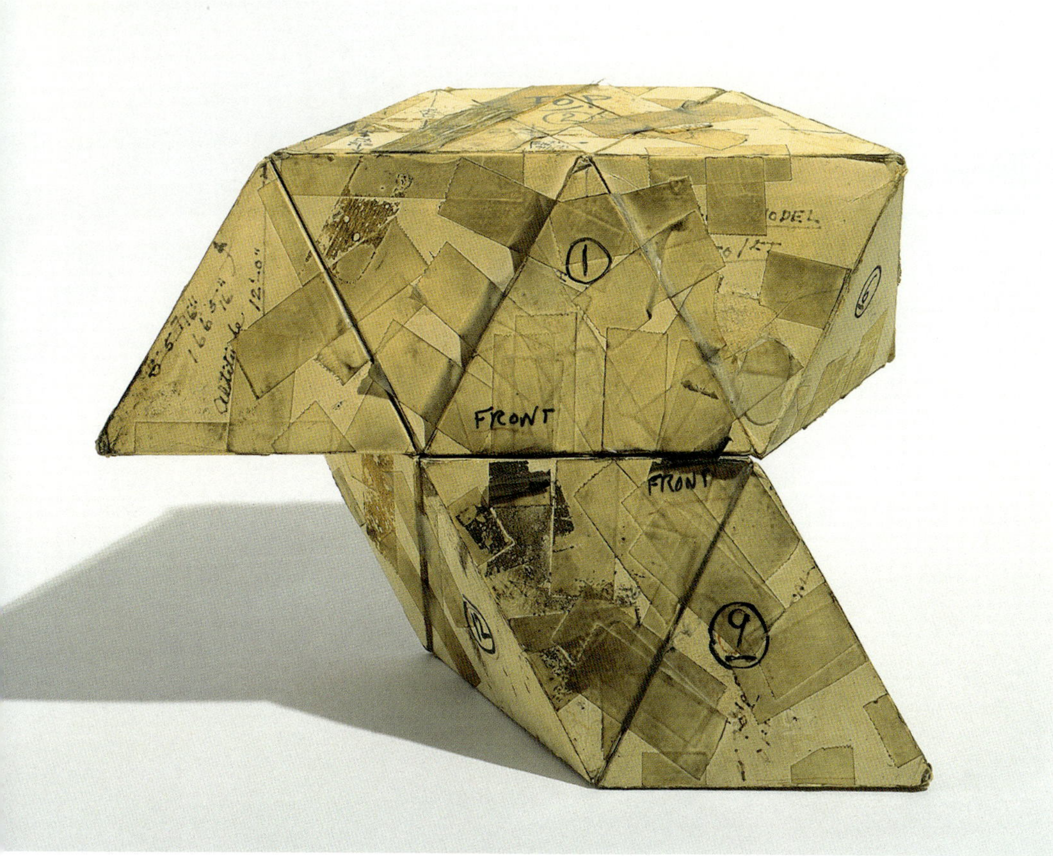

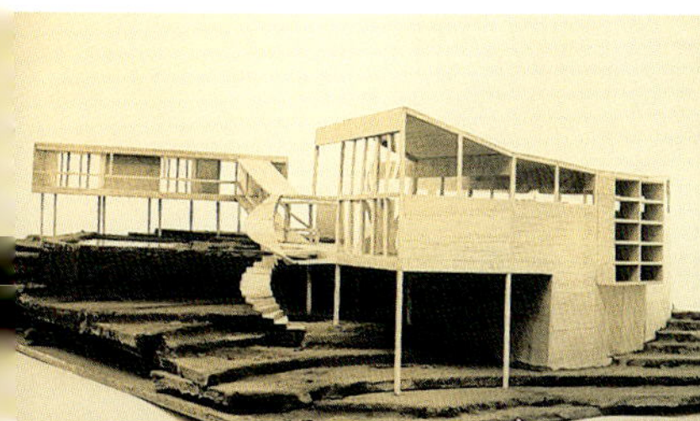

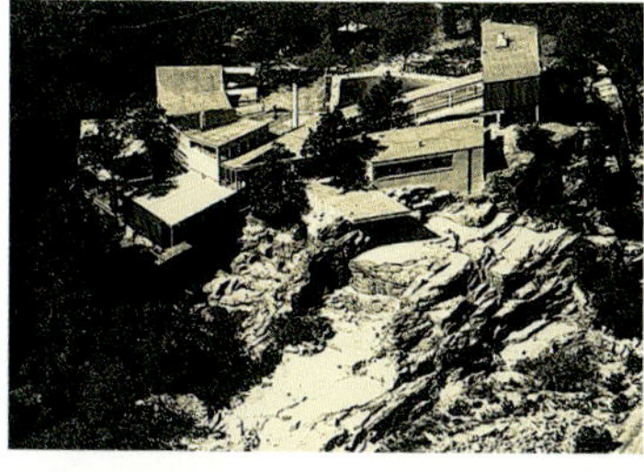

TONY SMITH
LEFT, MODEL FOR OLSEN HOUSE
RIGHT, OLSEN HOUSE, GUILFORD, CT,
COMPLETED 1953

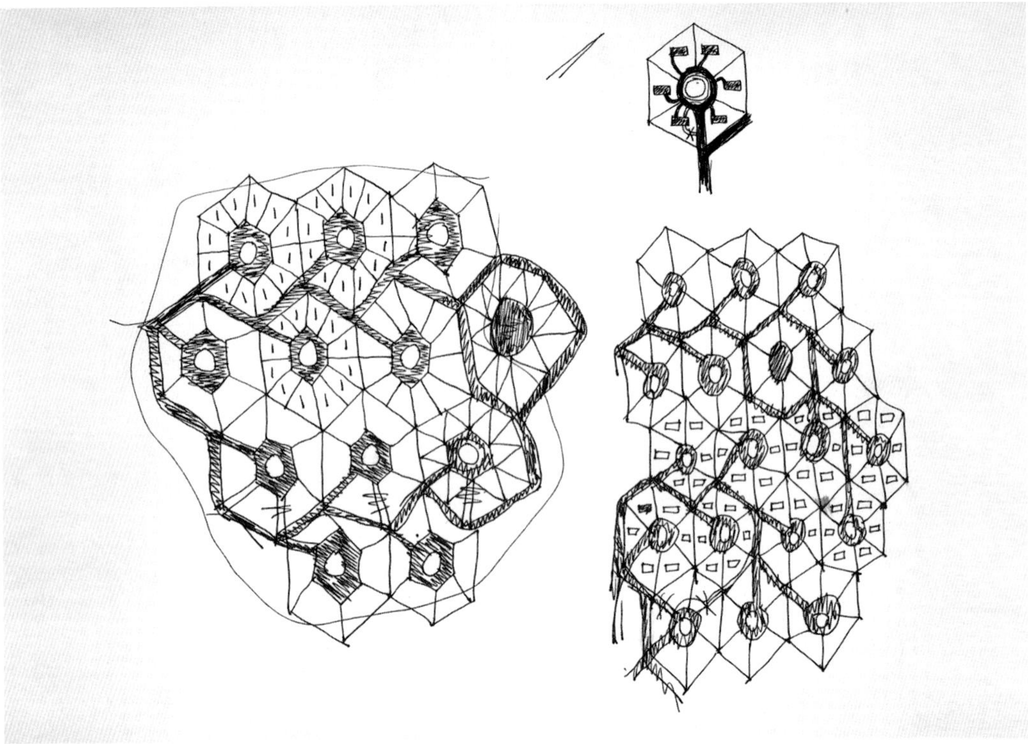

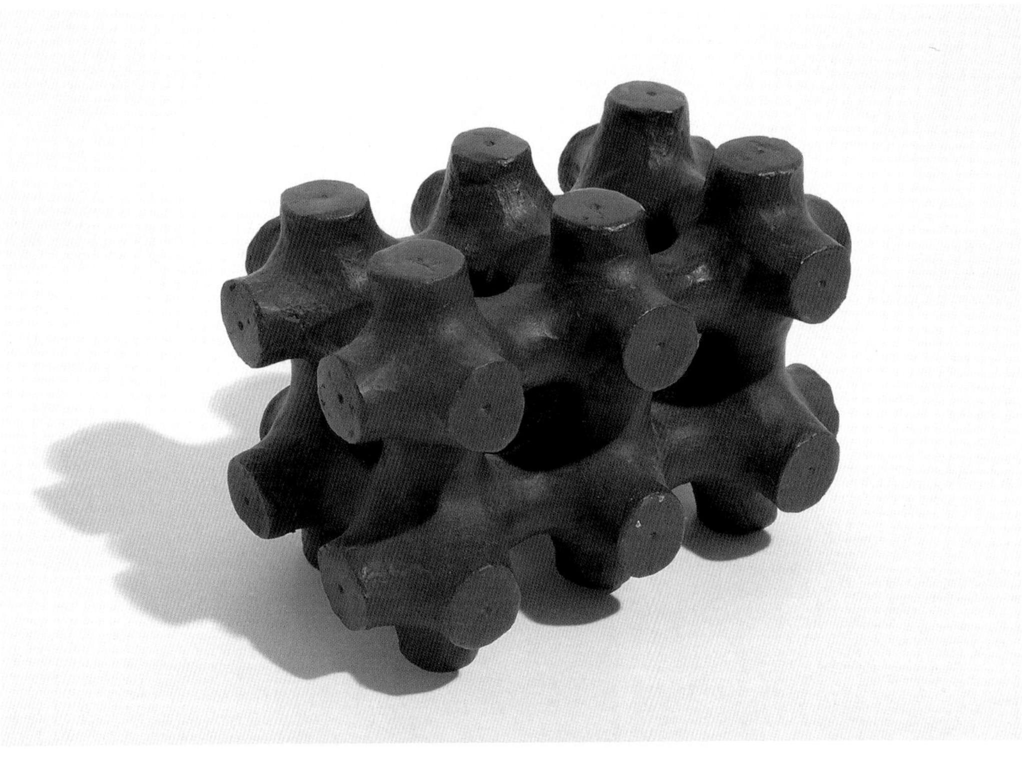

Plate List
Tony Smith

All artworks
© Tony Smith
Estate/Artists Rights
Society (ARS), NY
Images listed as
Collection of Tony Smith
Estate are Courtesy of
Matthew Marks and
Mitchell-Innes & Nash
Galleries

pages 13 and 35 top
Tau, 1961-62
Cardboard model
6 1/2 x 10 x 6 in.
Collection of Jane Smith

**pages 16 left small
image and 27**
Wingbone, 1962
Plaster
26 x 25 x 116 in.
Collection of Chiara
Smith

**pages 16 right small
image and 26**
Tetrahedron, 1961
Plaster
38 x 48 x 43 in.
Collection of Donald L.
Bryant, Jr. Family Trust

page 17
Yellowbird, 1971
Painted cardboard
model
6 x 9 x 3 1/4 in.
Private Collection

pages 22-23
Untitled 1-4, 1954
Charcoal on paper
17 3/8 x 12 1/8 in. each
(x4)
Collection of Tony Smith
Estate

pages 24-25
April 23, 1961, 1961
Ink on paper
8 7/16 x 10 7/8 in. each
(x12)
Collection of Tony Smith
Estate

page 28
Untitled, 1962-63
Oil on canvas
42 x 48 in.
Collection of Matthew
Marks and Mitchell-Innes
& Nash Galleries, NY

page 29
Untitled, c. 1960s
Gouache on paper
5 3/8 x 6 3/4 in.
Collection of Jane Smith

page 30
Light Box, 1961
Cast bronze, black
patina, Ed. 3/6
26 1/4 x 20 x 22 in.
Collection of Tony Smith
Estate

page 31
Cross, 1960-62
Cast bronze, black
patina, AP
32 x 32 x 32 in.
Collection of Tony Smith
Estate

page 32
The Fourth Sign, 1974
Cast bronze, black
patina
22 1/2 x 55 1/2 x 38 in.
Collection of Tony Smith
Estate

page 33
Source, 1967
Cast bronze, black
patina
12 1/2 x 31 x 30 1/2 in.
Collection of IVAM
Centre Julio Gonzalez,
Valencia, Spain

page 34 top
Untitled, 1953-55
Charcoal on paper
31 3/4 x 39 1/4 in.
Collection of The
Museum of Modern Art,
NY

page 34 bottom left
Page from a sketchbook
c. 1945
Ink on paper
9 11/16 x 7 1/2 in.
Collection of Tony Smith
Estate

**page 34 bottom
center**
Olsen House (plan)
c. 1951
Pencil on paper
18 3/4 x 23 7/8 in.
Collection of Tony Smith
Estate

page 34 bottom right
My Blue Heaven (Olsen
House) c. 1951
Pencil on paper
18 1/8 x 24 in.
Collection of Tony Smith
Estate

page 35 bottom left
Model for Olsen House

page 35 bottom right
Olsen House
Guilford, CT, Completed
1953

page 36 top
Untitled (Plan for
Linear City), 1953-55
Ink on paper
11 x 13 7/8 in.
Private Collection, NY

**pages 36 bottom
and 100**
Fermi, 1973
6 1/4 x 9 x 6 in.
Cast bronze
Private Collection, NY

page 41
Throne, 1956-57
29 x 39 x 32 in.
Collection of Tony Smith
Estate

pages 42-43
Bryant Park, NY, 1967
Artist pictured with
plywood maquette of
Willy
Photograph by David
Gahr

page 44
Die, 1962
72 x 72 x 72 in.
Steel with oiled finish
Collection of Paula
Cooper

pages 46-47
Bryant Park, NY, 1967
Artist pictured with
plywood maquette of
Night
Photograph by David
Gahr

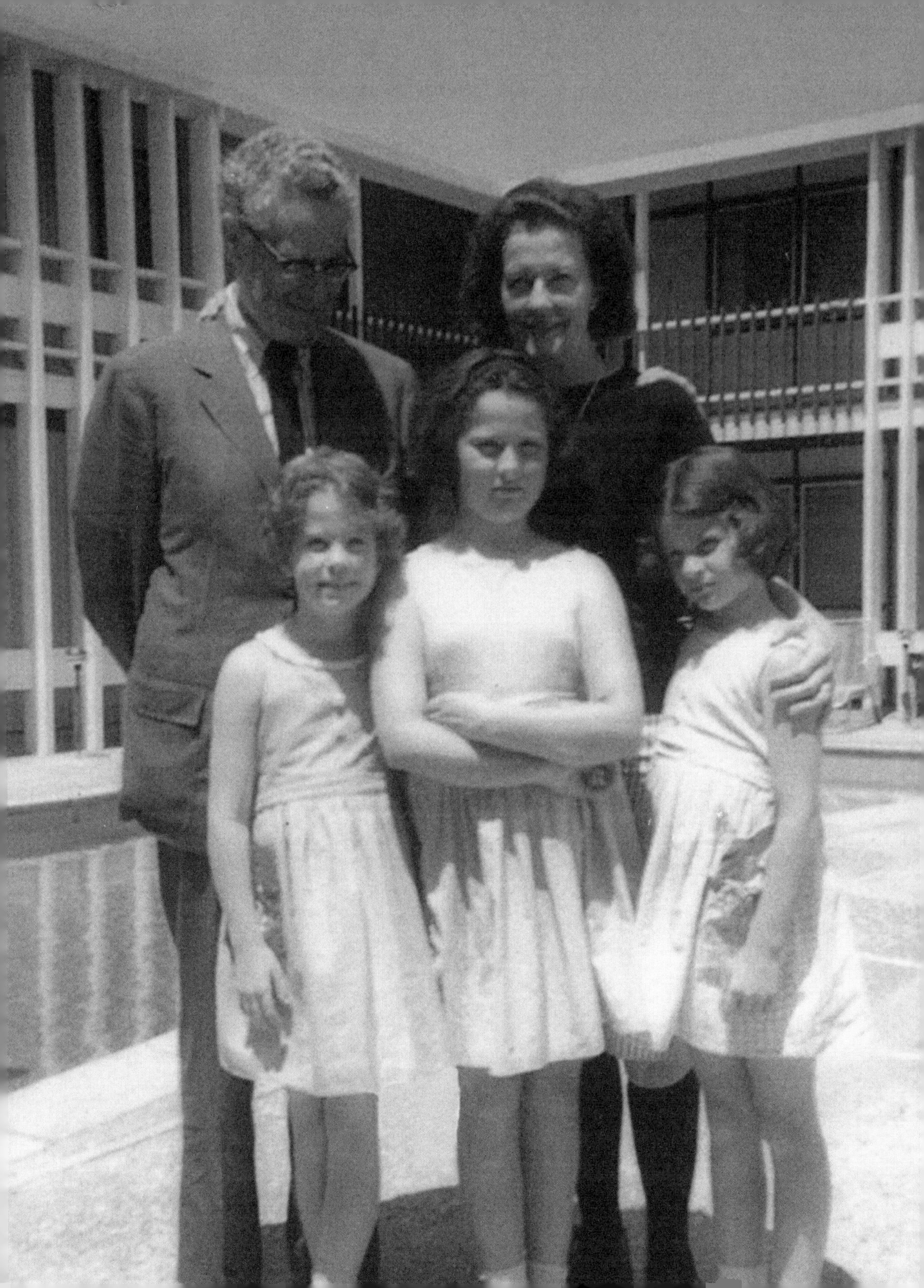

There Was a Family Named Smith
by Gilbert Brownstone

What is the relationship between art and family? In the Brueghel dynasty of thirteen successive painters Pieter Brueghel the Elder (c. 1525-1569) is probably the most famous, though two of his sons, Peter Brueghel the Younger (c. 1564-1638) and Jan Brueghel I (c. 1568-1625), are also acknowledged artists. Jan II (c. 1601-1678) took over his father's studio, while his son, Abraham Brueghel (c. 1631-1697), pursued his art career in Italy. There are other dynasties, too. Both Hieronymus Bosch's grandfather and his father were renowned painters. We are aware of monumental 20th century artist Alexander Calder, but may not know his father Alexander Stirling Calder, and his grandfather Alexander Milne Calder, both sculptors, whose works adorn Philadelphia's historic downtown and City Hall. Then there are the Dufy brothers, Raoul and Jean, and the Giacomettis, not to mention the Wyeths.

With the Smiths, Tony, Kiki and Seton, we have another case of art running in families, though the independence with which these three artists have pursued their careers presents an intriguing case. Painter, sculptor, architect, and forerunner in the Minimal art movement, Tony Smith inspired artists such as Carl Andre, Donald Judd, and Sol LeWitt. Kiki Smith uses a broad array of media to explore the human body and the natural world, and Seton's photography interrogates the relationship between architectural and human scale. Perhaps out of a desire to succeed on their own terms, the daughters have never affiliated themselves with their father's work, been represented by his galleries, or participated in joint exhibitions. *The Smiths* is the first time their works have been shown together. The intent of this exhibition is to present the works of Tony, Kiki and Seton Smith together in order to open new readings of the works by exploring the links – familial, thematic, material – between them.

SMITH FAMILY PHOTOGRAPH, 1963
ROW 1, LEFT TO RIGHT: SETON, KIKI, BEBE
ROW 2, LEFT TO RIGHT: TONY, JANE

The studio-house

I was fascinated to learn when interviewing Kiki, Seton, and Tony's wido, Jane, how the practice of art was integrated into everyday life in their household.

Jane, an opera singer and theater actress, toured Europe in the 1950s, and was singing at the Heidelberg Opera in 1953 when Tony moved to Germany to join her. Their first daughter Chiara (Kiki) was born in Nuremberg in 1954. In May 1955 they returned to the United States and settled in the small, middle-class town of South Orange, N.J., in the house where Tony was born. Twin girls, Seton and Beatrice (1955–1988), were born in July. Tony, who worked as an architect before devoting himself fully to sculpture in 1960, began to explore different artistic practices at this time, such as painting and the construction of geometric forms like cubes, tetrahedrons, octahedrons, and dodecahedrons. His first sculpture, *Throne*, dates from 1956-57.

Away from New York's cultural bustle, the family home became a studio for Tony and a rehearsal space for Jane. Kiki, Seton, and Beatrice (who followed her mother into music) grew up in a uniquely rich cultural context, surrounded by the sound of their mother's vocal practice and the shapes of their father's architectural models and sculptures. The children were influenced by this fertile creative environment and seem to have been shaped by exposure to the idea that creativity is part of everyday life.

The children assisted Tony in his work. Jane remembers: "He started making little dodecahedrons and tetrahedrons, and all the children in the neighborhood and the family were involved in making these little forms. Then Tony would assemble them according to what pleased him." Kiki speaks of "moving the sculptures around the backyard . . . the three of us like Egyptians. We helped him to build the models after school, and friends of ours came and helped us. I made the model for *Smoke*, maybe the first model."

Is it any wonder that neither Kiki nor Seton locate their artistic production within a studio environment? "I don't have a studio," Kiki says. 'I work in my living room as he did. We grew up with a model of an artist working at home and at the same time being able to produce large pieces of work. So we were both incorporated into that sort of practice."

The fact that Tony's studio was also his house allowed Kiki and Seton to be involved in an ongoing artistic apprenticeship. According to Jane, "They were surrounded by art. Tony wanted very much to honor the painters of that time. We had a Pollock painting, a Rothko painting and a Newman painting because he believed they were the most important painters of that time . . . and they were! So the children saw them on their walls. I remember one painting by Agnes Martin, an off-white painting with two rectangles on raw canvas. Seton said 'that is not something, it's just space,' and Agnes thought [the remark] was wonderful because it was really what her work is about!"

The Smiths' home became a busy center where friends met and exchanged ideas. Within their circle of friends and colleagues were writers, singers, musicians and painters, such as the famous Abstract Expressionists Mark Rothko, Jackson Pollock and Clyfford Still, whose careers Tony actively supported, and many other artists who took refuge with the family and participated in the beehive of activity in the "studio-house."

Mealtimes were very lively. Kiki remembers sitting at the dinner table as a child listening in on the conversations. Seton says: "Tony rarely went to visit people, so people came to visit us. Mark di Suvero and of course Barnett Newman. . . Chris Wilmarth was there, and various assistants over the time . . . in particular the painters Bob Swain,

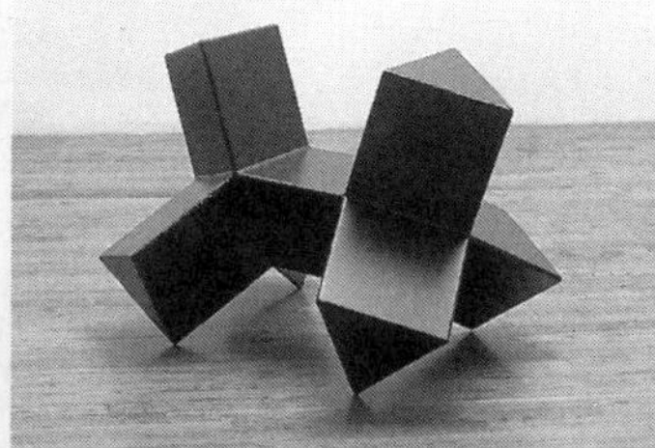

TONY SMITH
THRONE, 1956-57

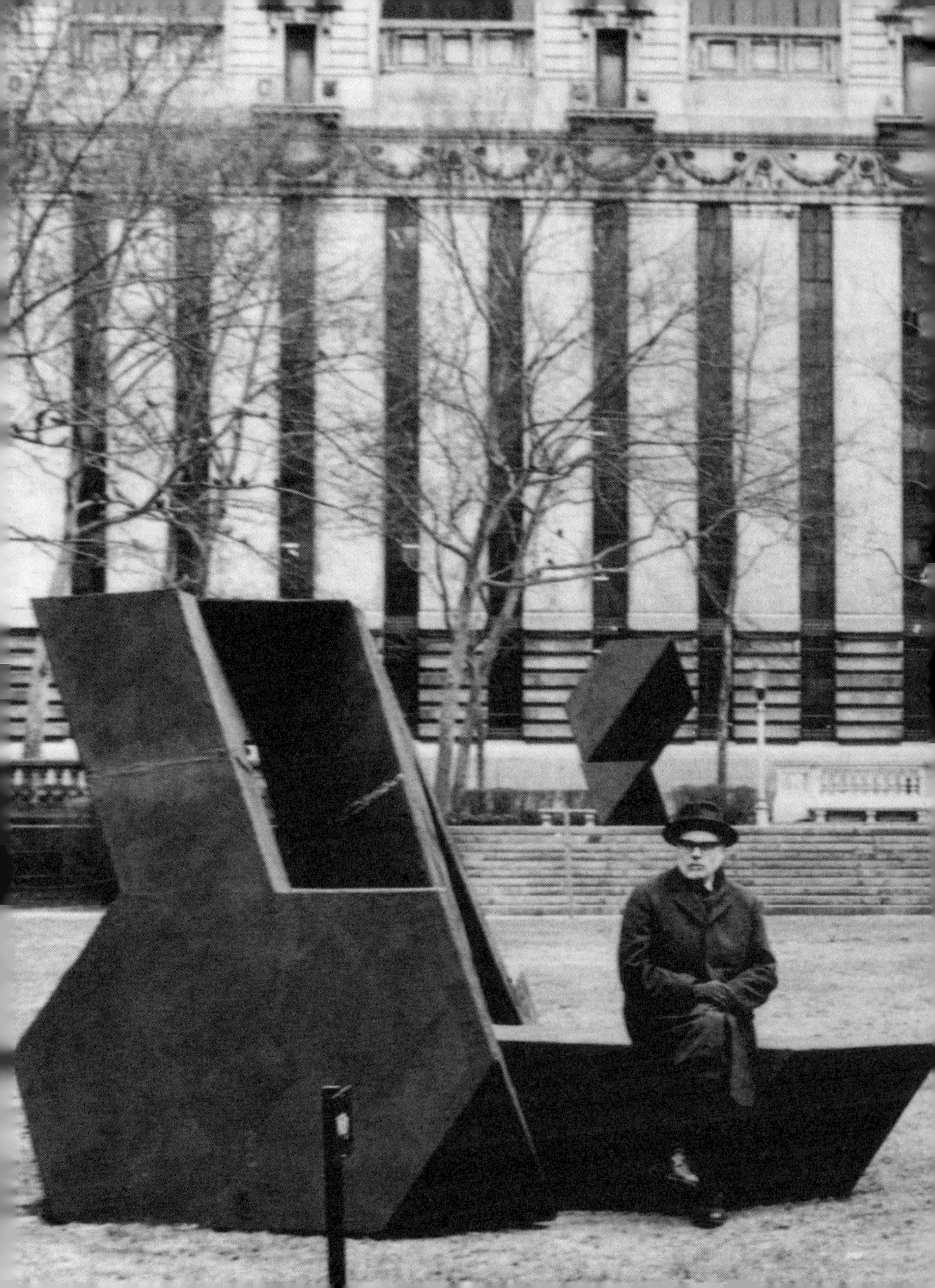

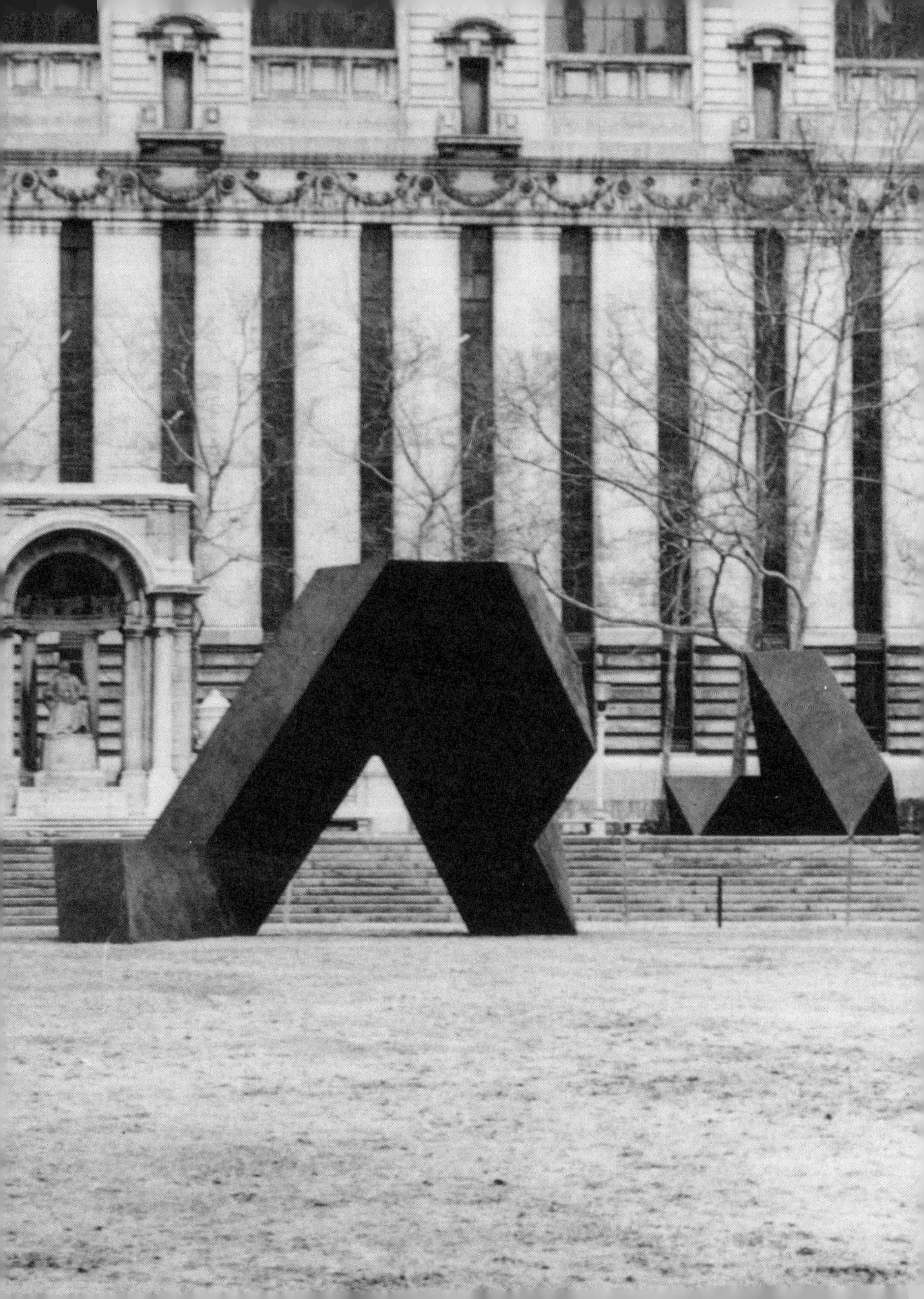

Jim Shepperd, Vincent Longo, Doug Ohlson, Sandy Wurmfeld. They became teachers at Hunter College, following in Tony's footsteps. I especially remember Scott Burton, Jean Dupuy, Sam Wagstaff, Robert Mapplethorpe and Richard Tuttle. They were a real cast of characters. So you can imagine what an unusual environment we were brought up in. And then Jane's side, of course. She had her friends, like Tennessee Williams, who were writers, that was part of her influence on us."

Undoubtedly their parents' strong artistic identities and the tenor of this intellectual circle influenced the girls. Seton recalls: "Jane was the actress, but I would say Tony was the drama in the house, reading *Finnegans Wake* and Ezra Pound up to late hours, so that was part of the house, with Jane singing and the fire going in the fireplace, and lots of alcohol. . . ."

This unusual mix of art and life forms the basis of Tony's influence on Kiki's and Seton's work. "I suppose that there were some amusements, but it was a pretty serious place! I mean, he was a kind of force, but the other people who visited us were also, and even if you might not understand everything (being a teenager), it was clear there were serious things going on there, and I think I was influenced by all this," remembers Seton.

Though many children are encouraged to paint and draw, it is clear that Kiki and Seton showed an aptitude for artmaking at an early age. Kiki recalls her sister's early interest in art: "Seton wanted to be an artist when she was about eleven or twelve or thirteen. She said she wanted to be an artist, whereas I did not really want to be an artist until I was about twenty-four or something like that. Seton copied my father making still life, and I sort of copied Seton making still life. And that is where I started out. When I was starting to make art I just drew still life for a year and a half, maybe

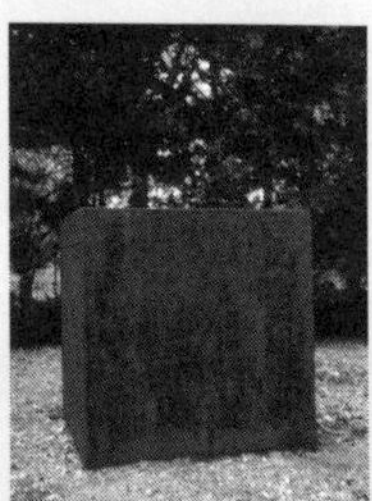

TONY SMITH
DIE, 1962

two. Seton had much more career sense of wanting to find herself as an artist."
For Seton "it was not a decision. I remember I was painting when I was young and
Tony recommended that I use acrylic because it was easy for a young person to use.
I bought pre-stretched canvases, nine by twelve inches, and I [couldn't wait] to leave
school to go home and paint. I was obsessed with different paintings."

In a text dating from 1993,[1] Seton describes with great sensitivity the disquieting
atmosphere of the "studio-house" in which she grew up: "The world in which we learn
to interpret symbols and sensations as children follows us, like the cold that pervaded
the house…. My personal past is inevitably mingled with my work even if it comes to
me in an obscured form, as in discovering the clues which surface and resonate one
after another…."

The cube as common denominator

Their divergent approaches might make it difficult to find overt connections between
Tony, Kiki and Seton's work, but a closer examination reveals surprising correspon-
dences among the three artists. In 1962 Tony Smith produced one of his most famous
pieces, *Die*. It is a steel cube measuring 183 centimeters, precisely the same meas-
urement as Le Corbusier's *modulor* and also that of Leonardo da Vinci's *Vitruvian
Man (The Proportions of the Human Figure.)* Like the Italian master, whose concern
was to fit the human body into the circle and the square, Tony Smith inscribes the
realm of the human within the shape of the cube. Viewers cannot take in the sight of
the cube except by stepping away from the object. They can then view its dimensions
in relation to their own scale. Thus, the cube rearticulates, in a new and striking

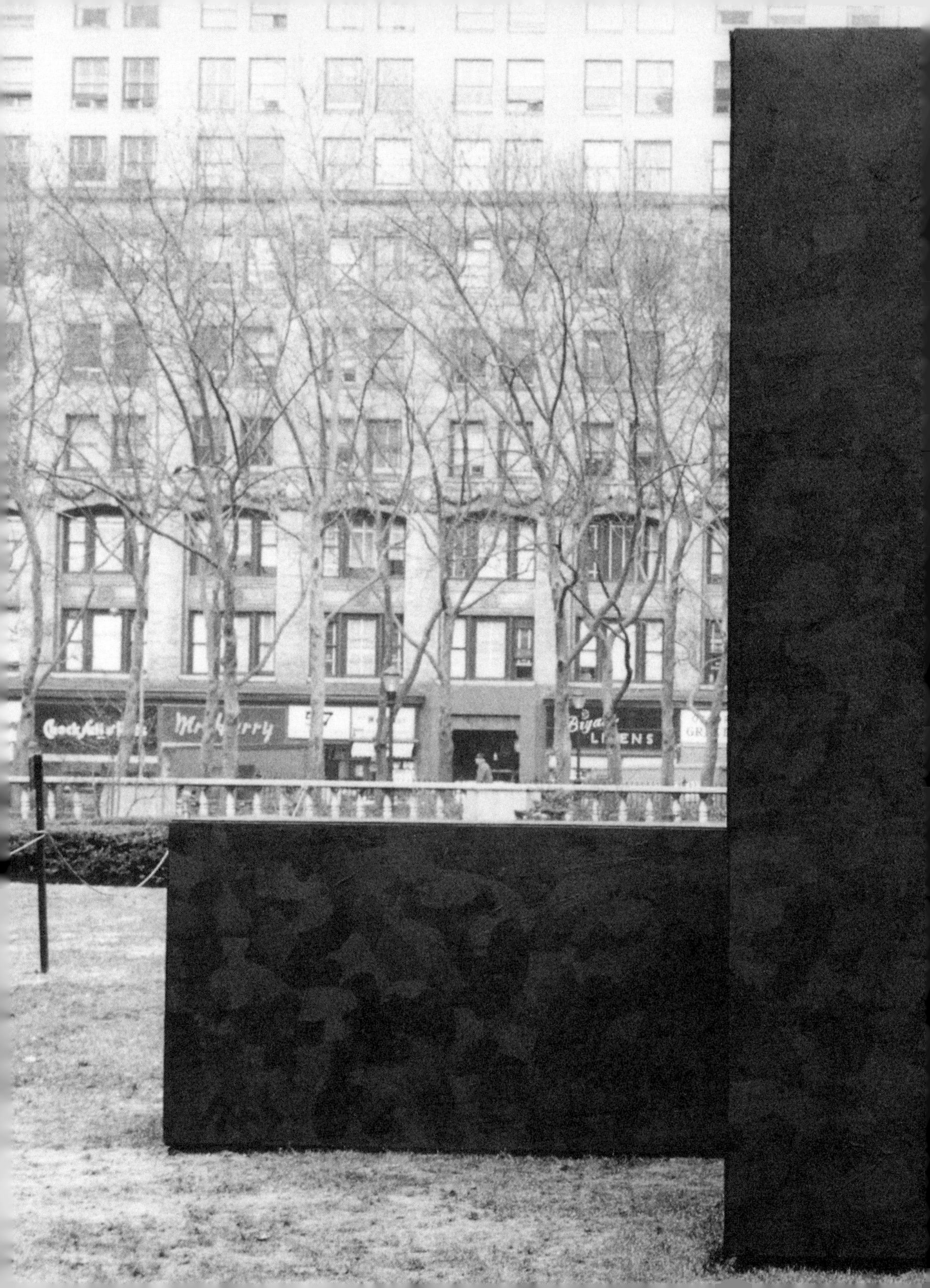
Mr Garry
957
Bryant
LINENS

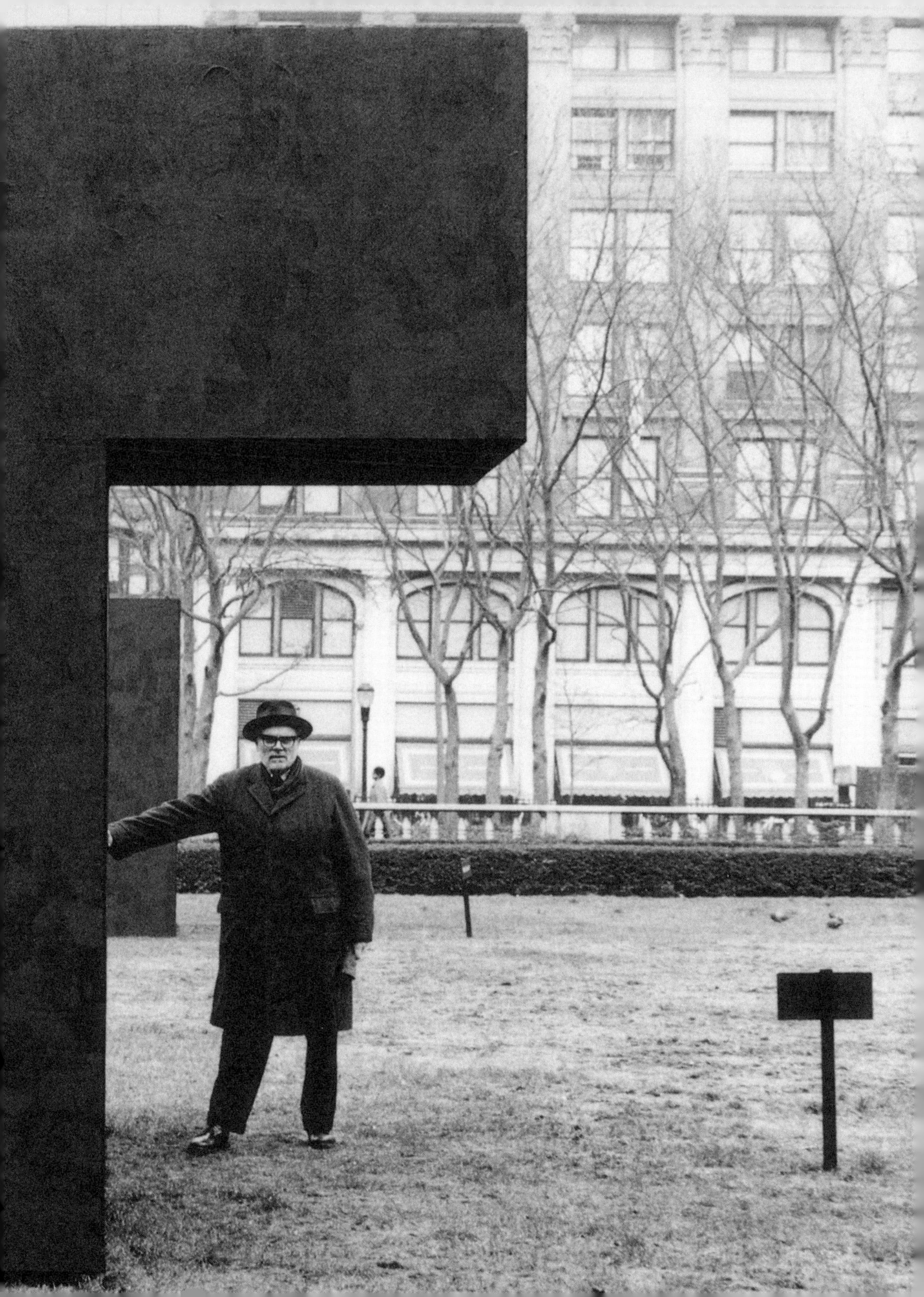

manner, the timelessness of the relationship between human beings and their world.

It seems this issue is engaged in each of the Smiths' work, as Kiki and Seton also approach the relationship between humanity and geometry, and the properties of human space: Kiki from the inside of the body – within the cube – and Seton from the outside, in the distance that separates us from the cube. One of the central concerns in Kiki's work is an exploration of human complexity, of mortality and organic form. In her art the body is more than a basic unit of matter that conforms to the laws of science. She gives the body a dimension that is political and social. Similarly, if human beings never appear in Seton's work, there is nevertheless a concern for them and their position in the world. The universe conjured by her photographs – of landscapes, architecture and interiors – are metaphors for what we are.

Kiki: "For me, I would say there are things that Seton and my father shared, and things that I shared with my father and with Seton. Like Seton definitely inherited the architectural side, and I probably just felt more the nature of my father's work. We both have different aspects of my father's and mother's interests we have incorporated into our own."

What would you see as a relationship?

Kiki: "In my work I have used images of small structures like cells or crystals to build a large whole, like the sperm piece that the Museum of Modern Art has. Using individual parts to make a whole probably comes from my father's work, and also using paper as a sculptural medium. My father was very hands-on in the model-making process, but then the fabrication was done in a foundry by welders. In my work I am still very hands-on, throughout most of the process."

What about the cube, Tony's cube, as a symbolic representation?

Kiki: "I think it is related to Leonardo's figure; it's an abstraction of the human figure in a certain kind of way. I talked about it as a coffin in the backyard where we are all going to go. But I don't know if it is something I consider in my work as a reference to making figurative work. I certainly see it as a successful sculpture. I very much like the concreteness and the eccentricities of my father's works, that they have a kind of cool, organic structure, but then they are extremely expressive and very individual, made by an individual, a specific personality."

Could you say that if you work within the cube, where we would stand, your sister Seton works outside the cube because her work has to do with architecture?

Kiki: "You can say that! It's not something I feel the necessity to analyze, nor does my personality take me there to analyze what it means. . . . I think that the relationships are just sort of there, and you can try to make sense of them . . . ."

How do you interpret Seton's work?

Kiki: "I think that Seton was much more conscious about architecture and architectural space and design. She is much more developed into space. I think that there is a relationship to my father's [art], and my father's work as an architect; it was always her interest. When she first started she was making work like photographing building sites, and then she made, for years, paintings of architectural spaces, furniture, images of interior spaces. She traveled a lot, looking at different forms of architecture, [and considering] what they mean emotionally . . . . It is not a neutral space, which I relate to very much in her work. It seems directly linked to our childhood, the house we grew up in. It has moods, an atmosphere that is familiar to me."

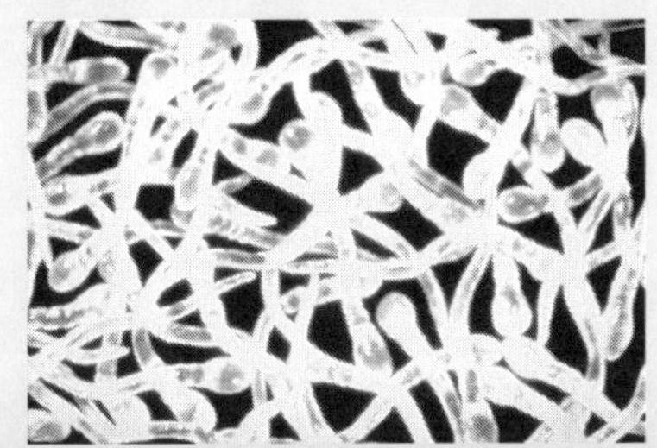

KIKI SMITH
UNTITLED (SPERM), 1989-90

Seton: "I think my work moved from a preoccupation with color and interiors to investigating architecture. When I was in college, I was introduced to the world of art history in a larger sense, including architectural history. At that time, American artists were making earthworks. I was fascinated by the wide variety of cultural and symbolic meaning that architecture seemed to propose as a language."

You could have been an architect?

Seton: "I am interested in creating site-specific projects for public spaces with the complexities of their social ramifications."

You come from the same cell; both of you were influenced by this presence in Tony's work?

Seton: "He taught us to consider the qualities of different materials and to look at almost everything as a potential resource. The other important issue was scale, through his work with models. The idea of a limited number of elements combined to create whatever arrangement was needed seemed to afford endless possibilities. I also discussed with him the properties of color. Tony, from an intellectual standpoint, encouraged us to rely on our own intuition. Our house was sparsely furnished, with not much more than folding tables and chairs. In retrospect, my way of viewing interiors as movable theater sets comes from there. This in turn plays a part in creating installations, as well as the notion of seeing objects and furniture as having presence."

And the cube?

Seton: "When I started making models for installations, it seemed natural that their sizes corresponded with those of standard building materials. Likewise, the scale of my photos has been related to standards such as 180 by 120 centimeters, for example, which is representative of human scale and suggestive of real architectural scale.

I think it was important for Tony how his work related to the natural environment. *Die* is particularly complex as it refers clearly to death and monumentality and perhaps to something eternal."

Kiki: "Tony was my model for being an artist in his devotion, perseverance, and commitment to his vision and how it defines one's daily life."

With his basic steel cube Tony Smith invites interpretation, suggesting that we are free to see in it what we wish. Here we are free to connect the lives of the Smiths or to keep them separate; to see their works as individual parts comprising a whole, as in Kiki's cells and crystals, or even as different faces of the same cube. Maybe we are invited to view the "studio-house" as a metaphor for the human activity unfolding within it, just as Seton uses the architectural model to express the scale of the human. Or maybe it is the experimental nature of art that links Tony, Kiki and Seton, and the revelation that the cube is not sealed, that we are free to open it, to go in, to move around.

Gilbert Brownstone, currently based in Paris, is a former curator at the Paris Museum of Modern Art and the Israel Museum in Jerusalem.

Translated from French by Anne Anthony
1 Seton Smith, Notes, "Cinq intérieurs= la maison, 1993," in *Seton Smith*, exhibition catalogue, Centre d'Art de Fréjus, Le Capitou, ed. Le Capitou, Fréjus et Electa, Milan, 1995, pp. 115-116.

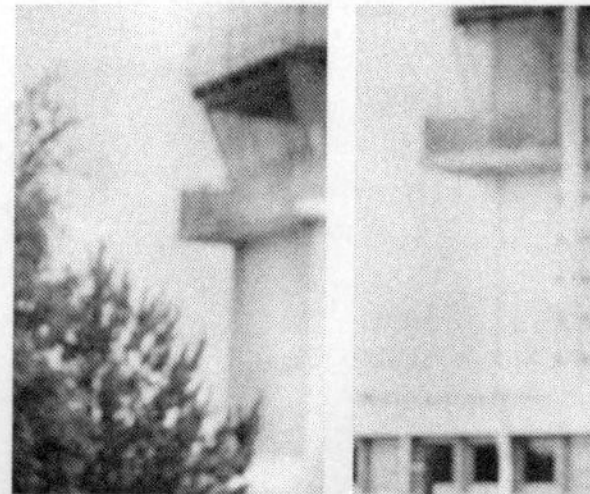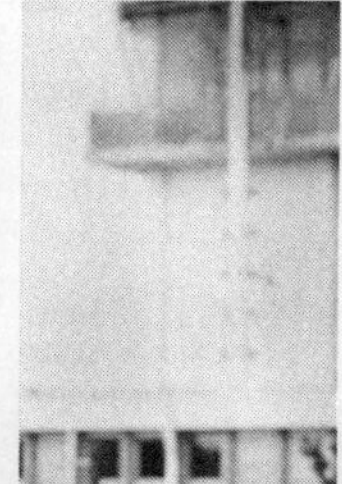

SETON SMITH
FROM TOWER TO TOWER, 1995

SMITH
SETON
SMITH

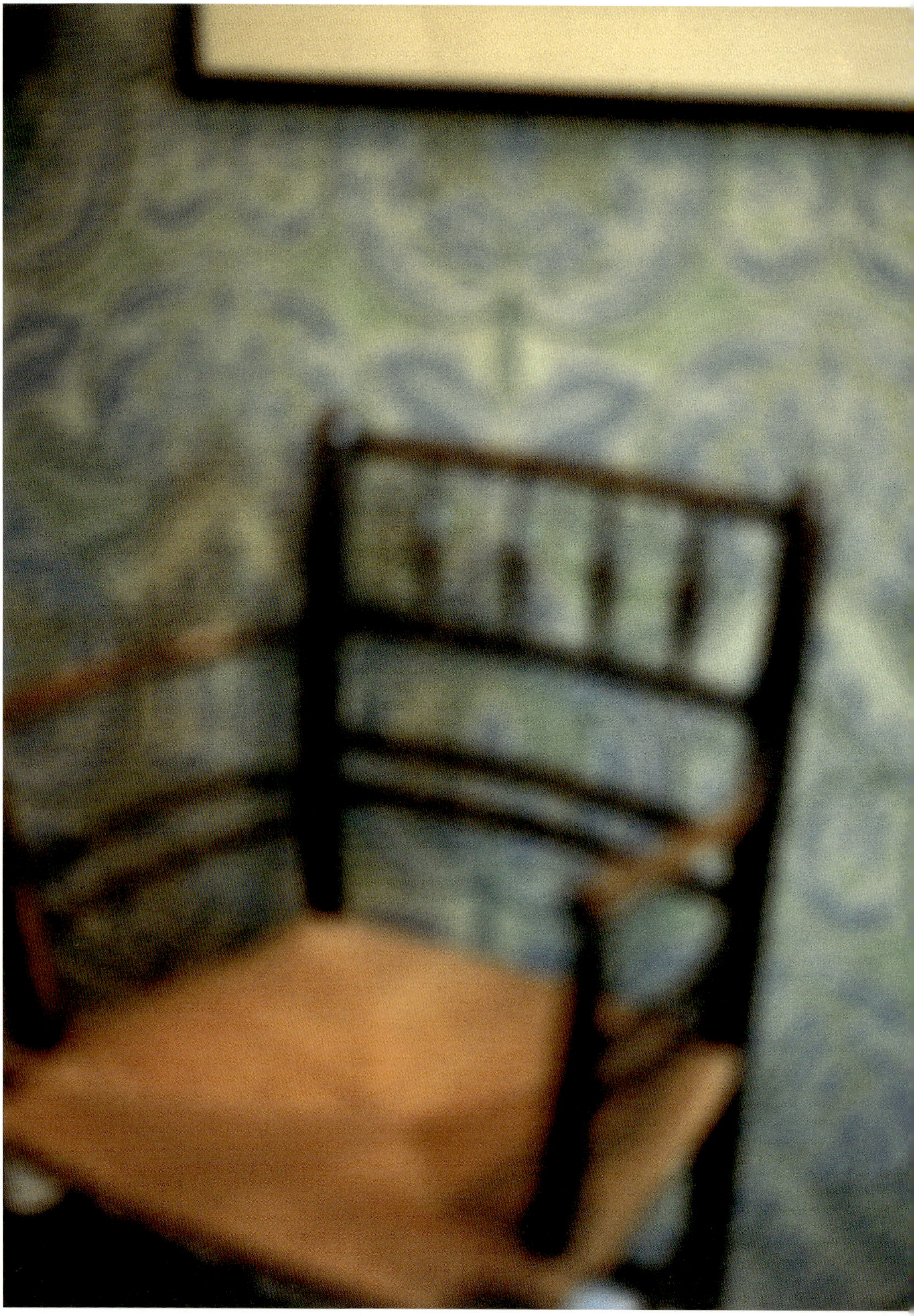

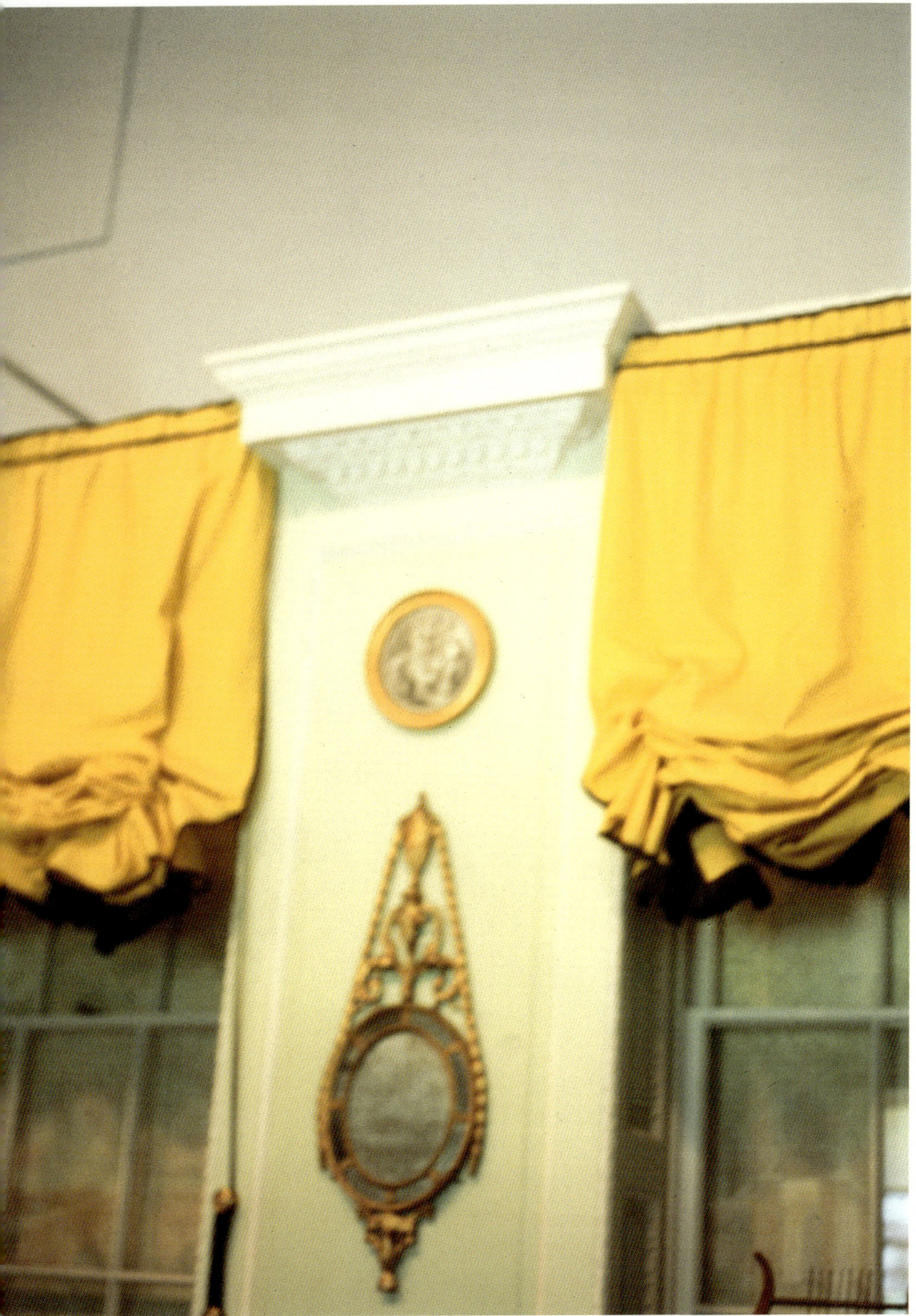

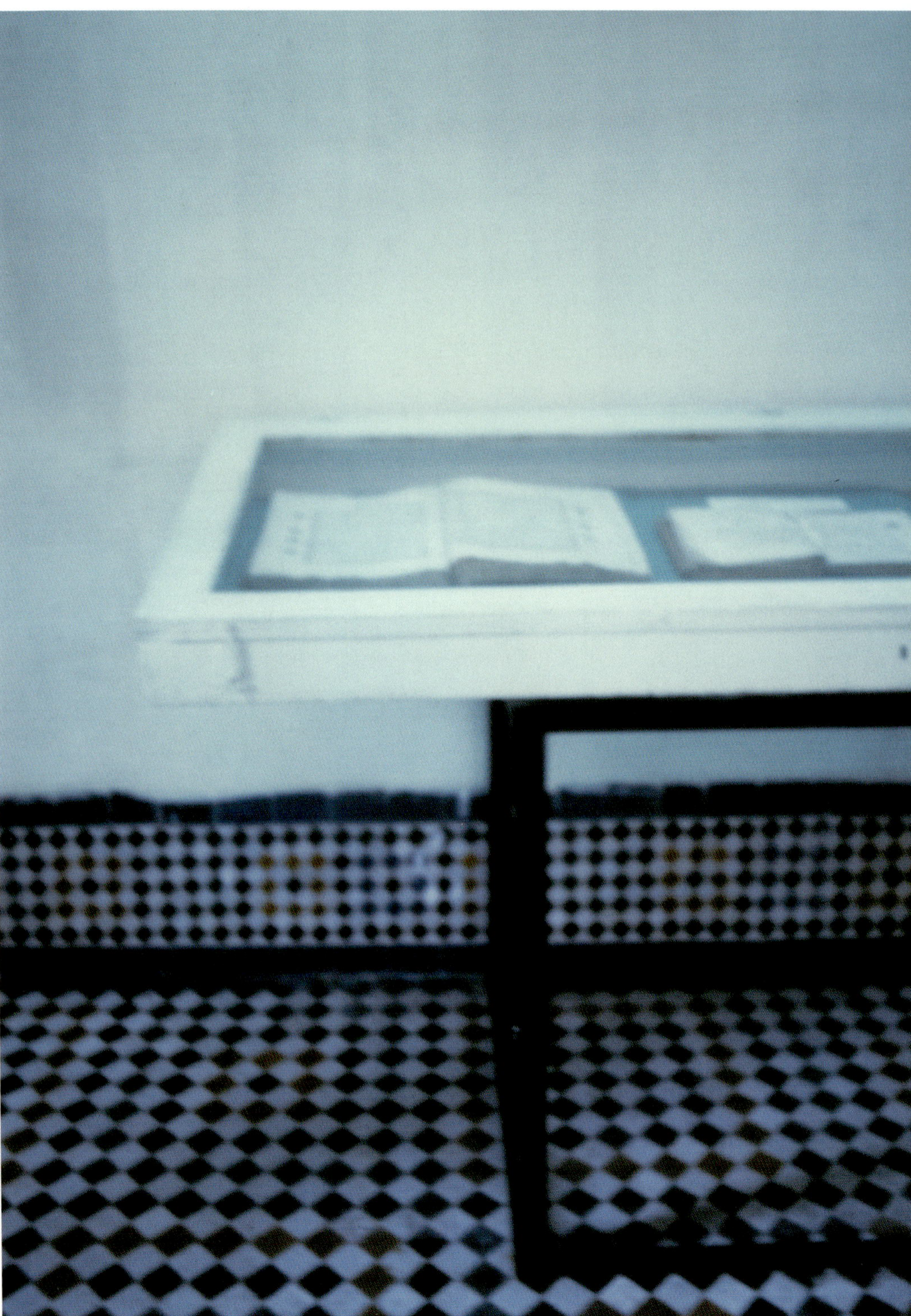

SETON SMITH, *FEZ CABINET*, 1997

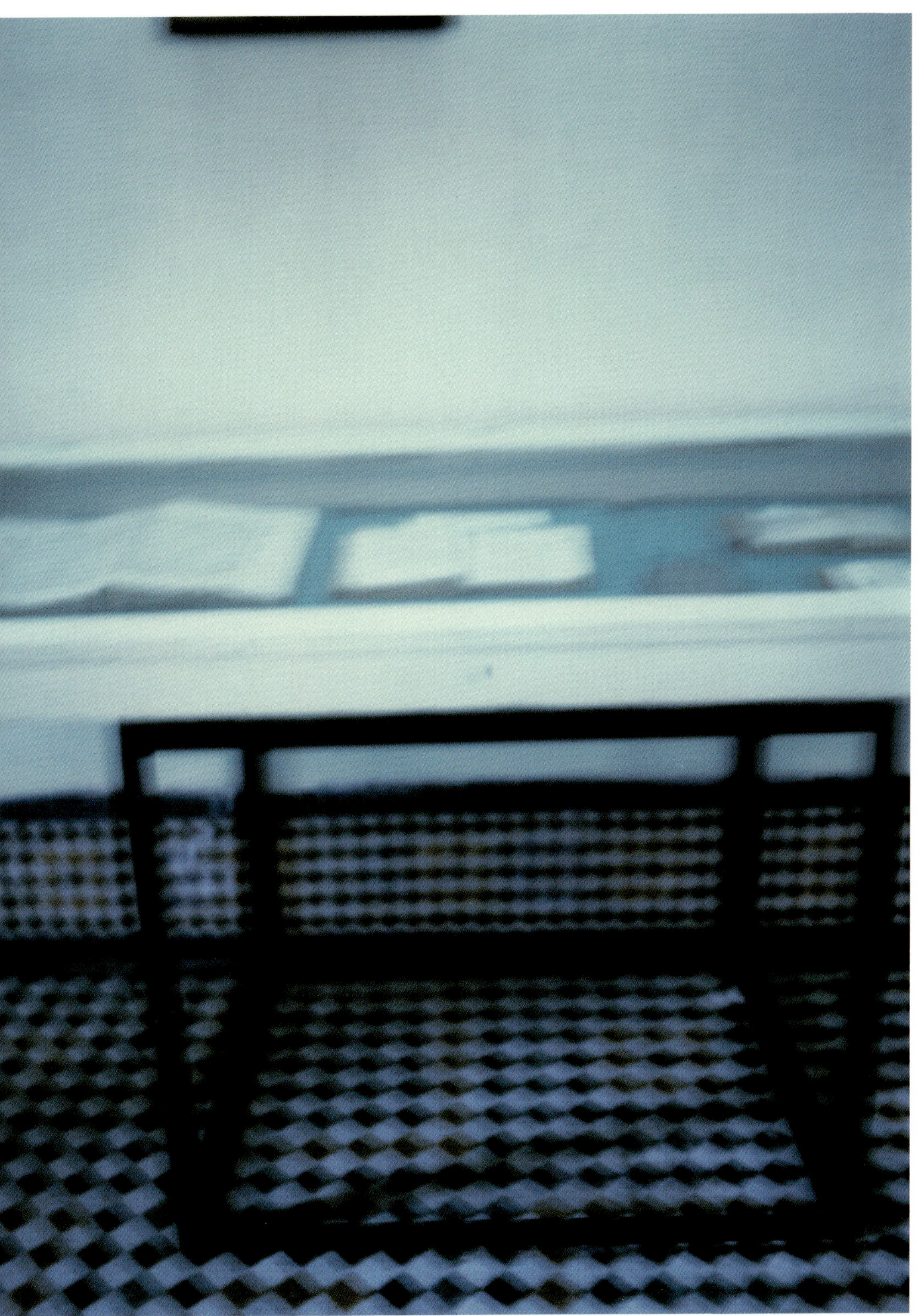

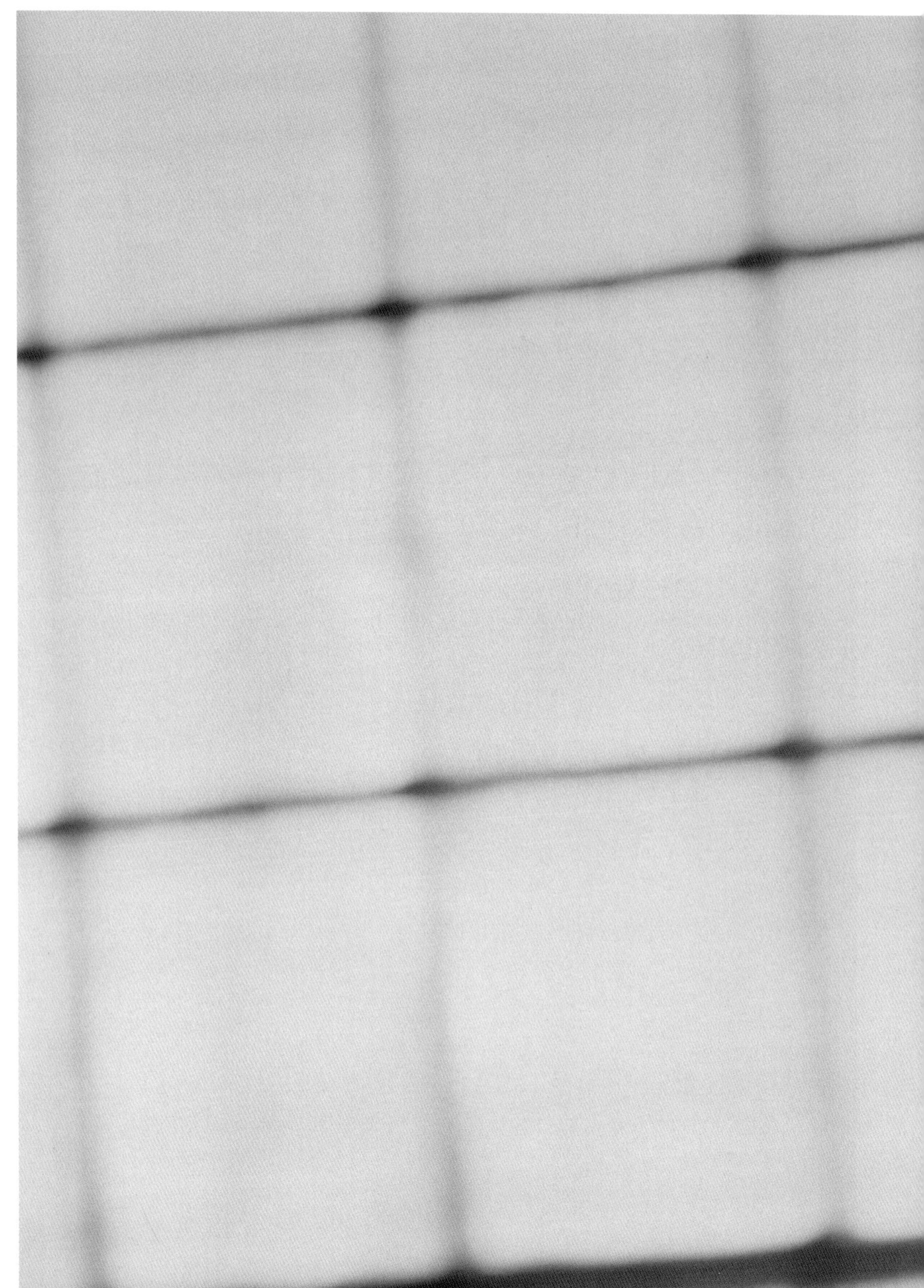

SETON SMITH, *WINDOW & BED* (FROM *WINDOWS FROM A CLEAR*), 1997

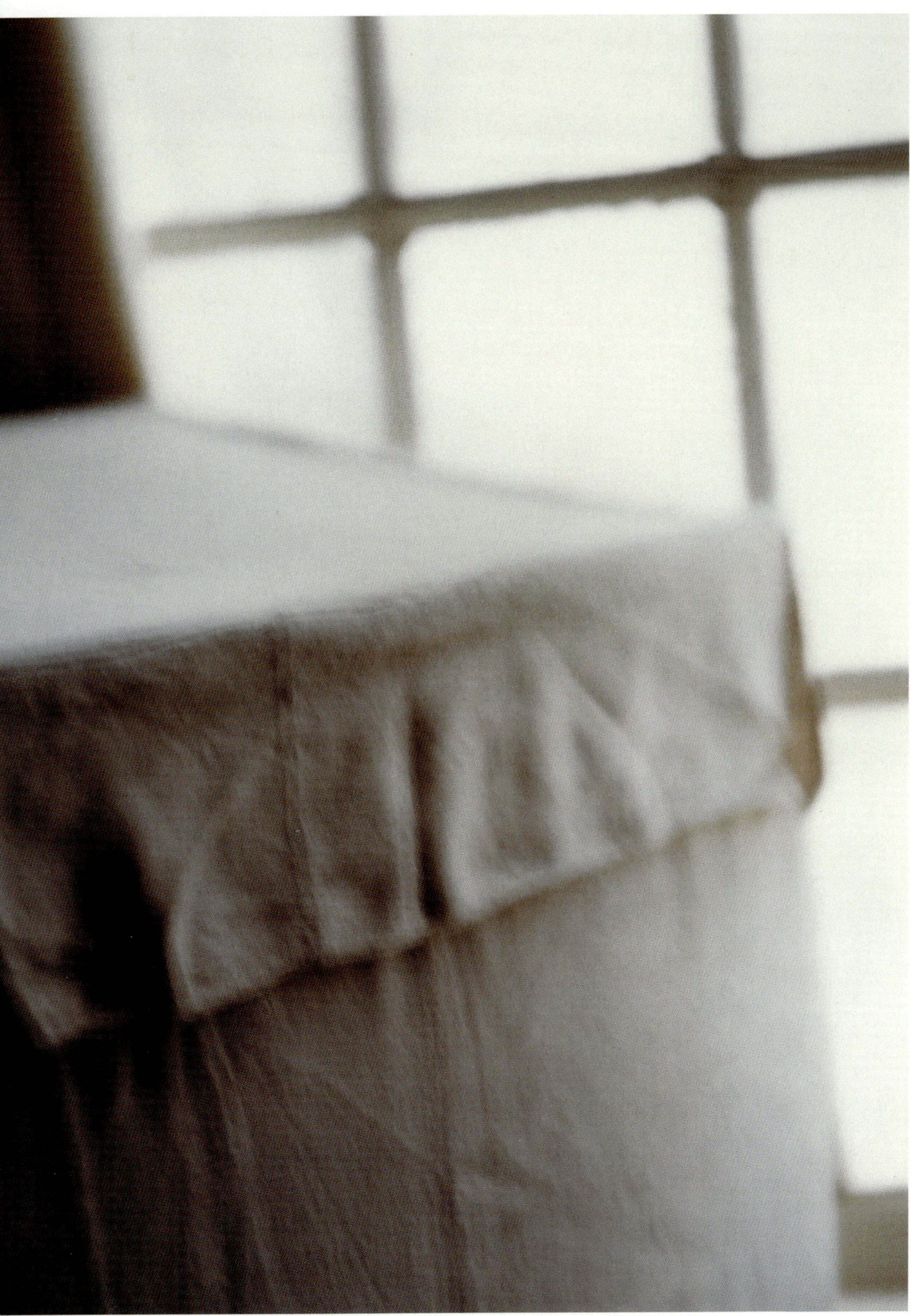

SETON SMITH, *LAMP, CABINET AND TABLE* (FROM *CHEZ P.S.*), 2000

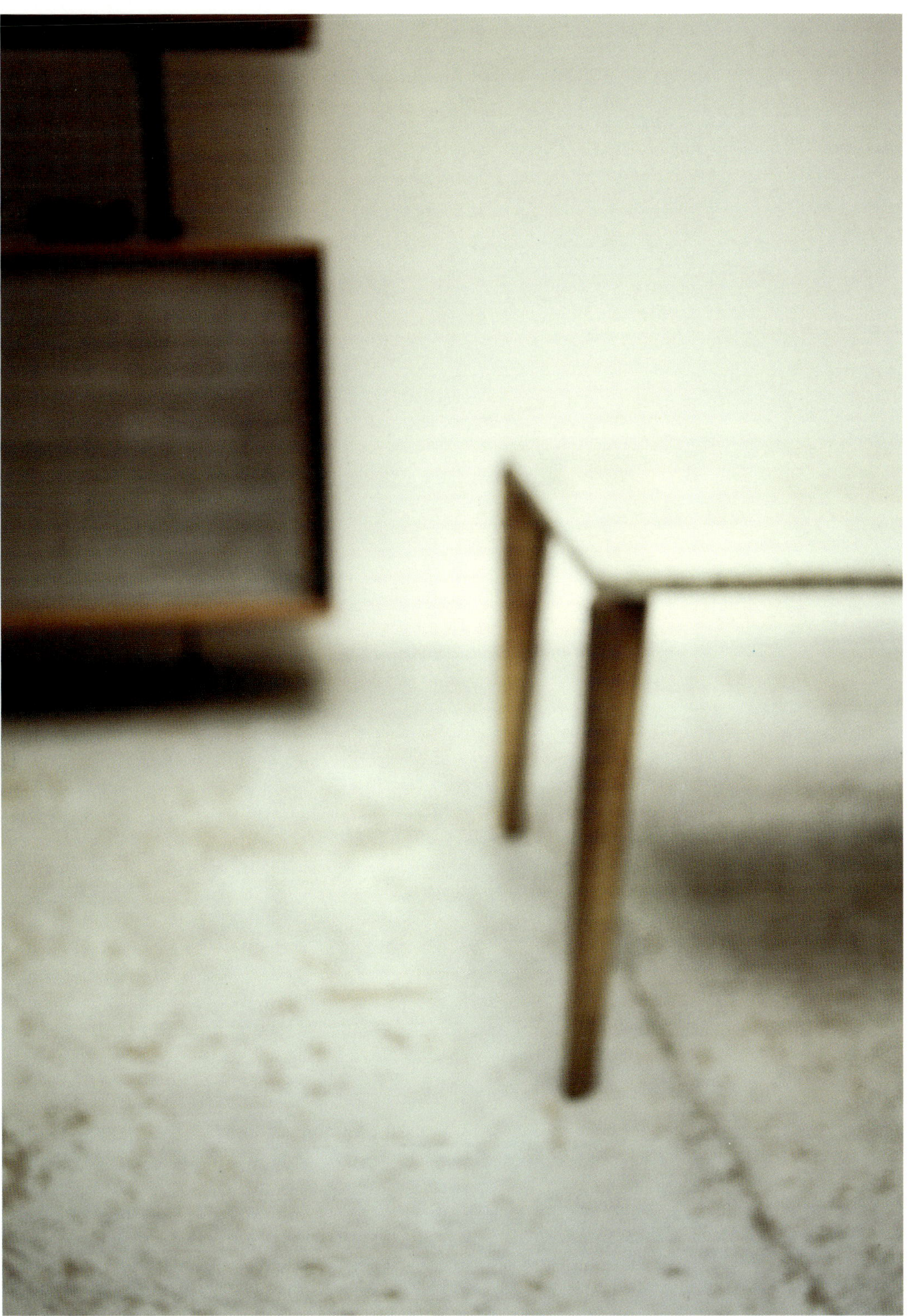

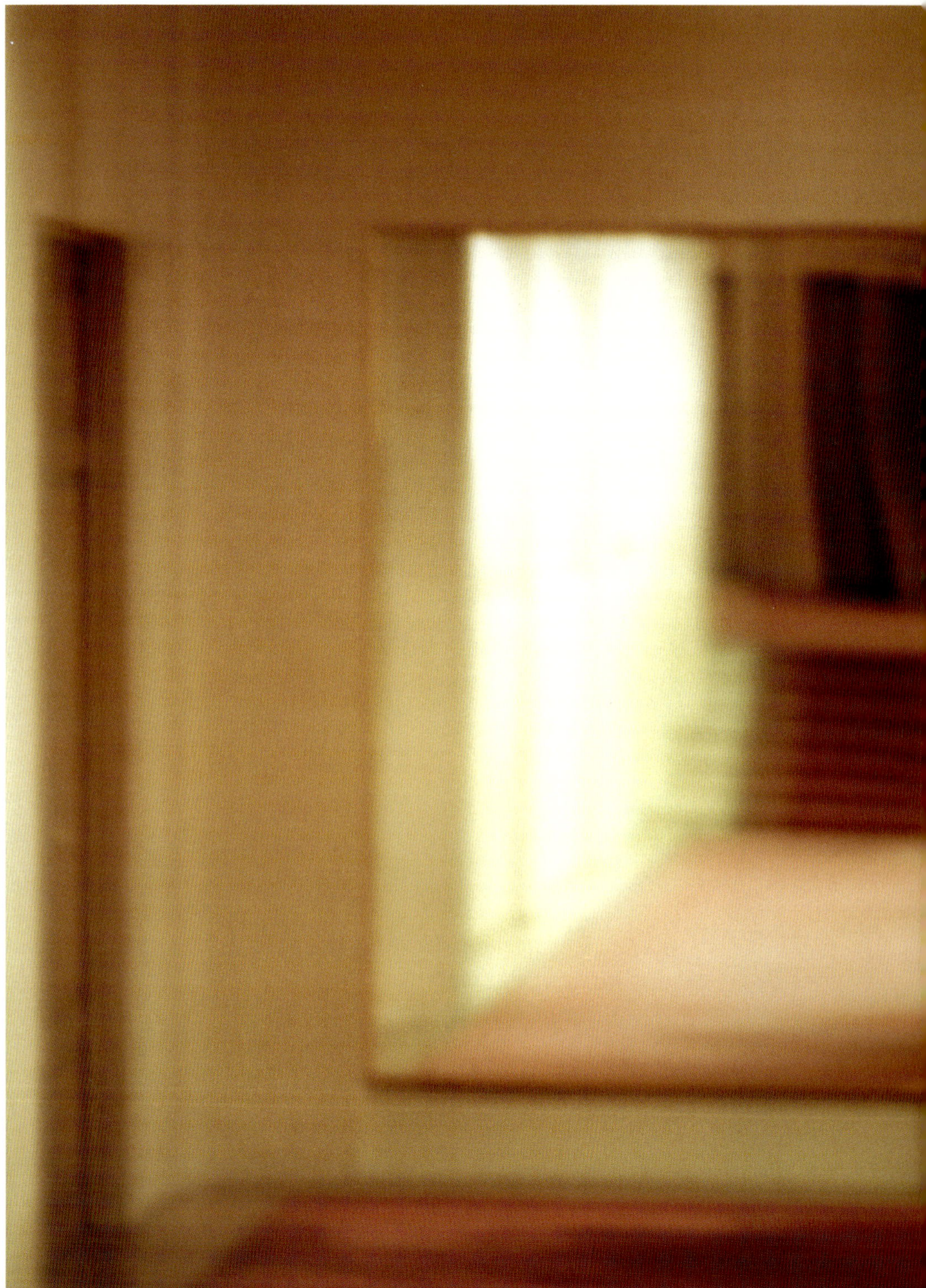

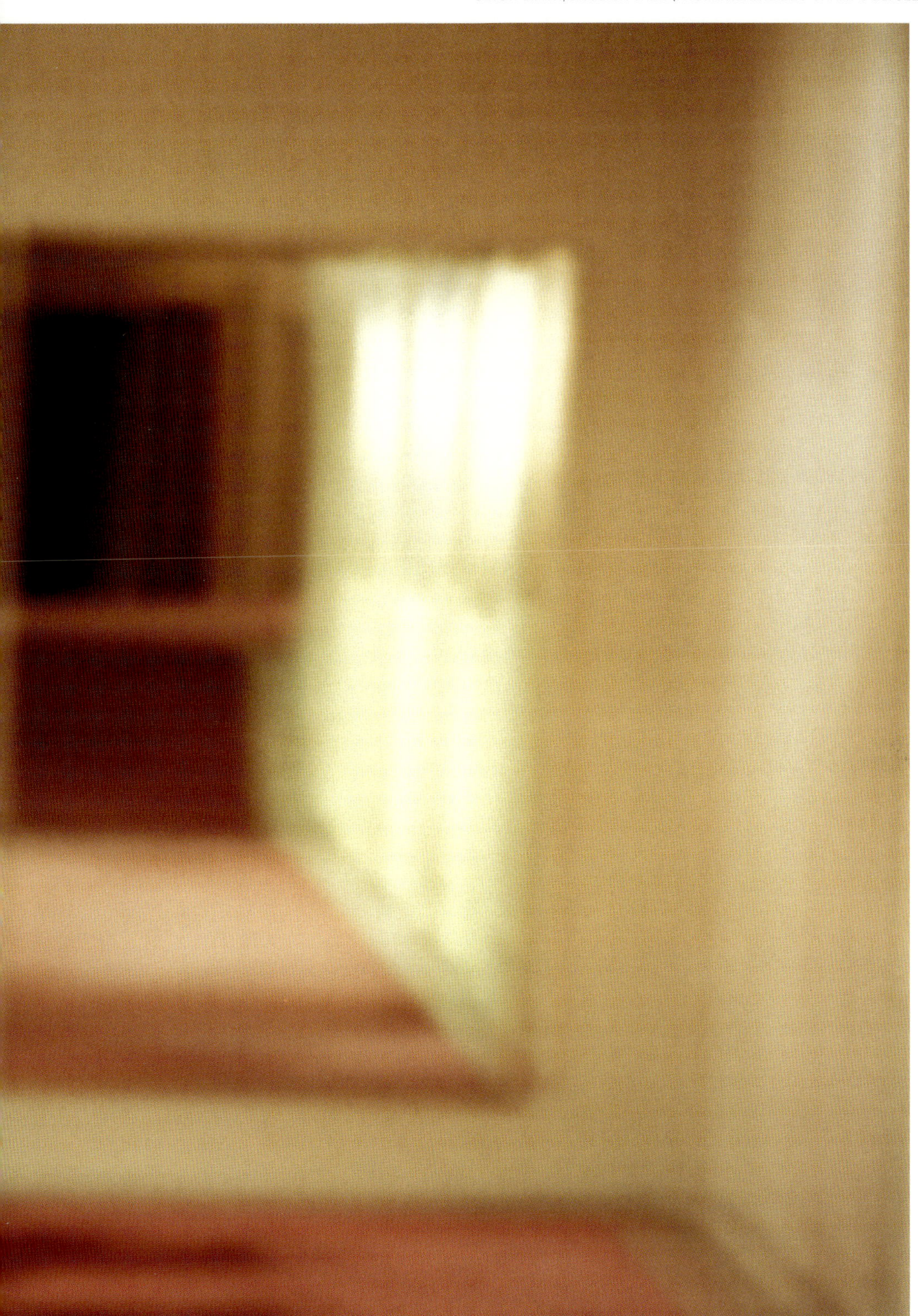

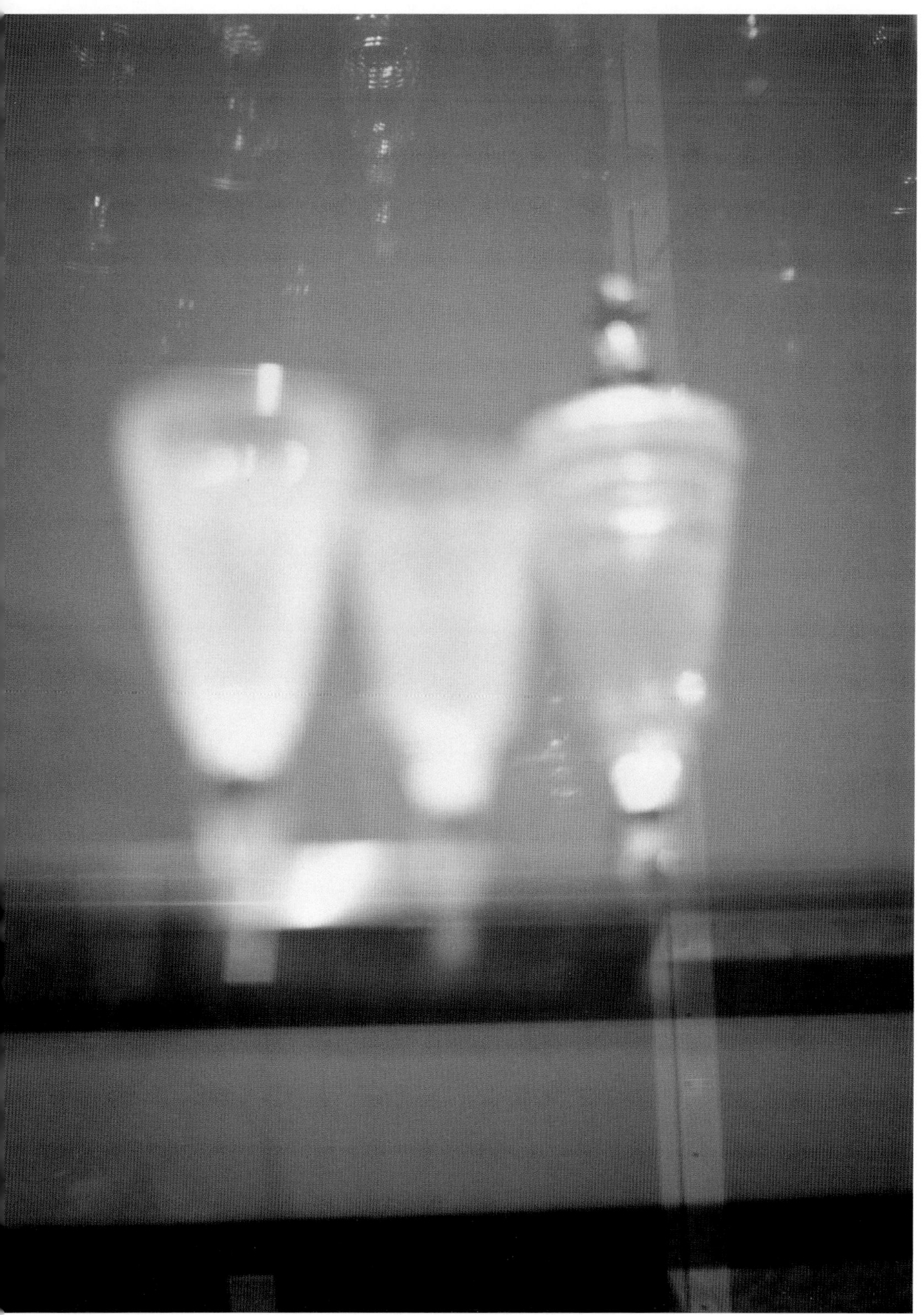

68/69

Plate List

Seton Smith

All images © Seton
Smith

**pages 14-15 left to
right**
*Lamp, Cabinet and
table, Cabinet with black
vases, Little lamps,
Cabinet with table II*
(from *Chez P.S.*), 2000
Cibachrome
72 x 48 in. each
Collection of the artist

page 51
From Tower to Tower,
1995
Cibachrome
72 x 48 in. each, diptych
Courtesy of Winston
Wächter Mayer, New
York

pages 54-55
*Spindle Chair with Blue
Wallpaper and Yellow
Curtains with Oval
Mirror* (from *English
Series*), 1993
Cibachrome
72 x 48 in. each, diptych
Collection of the Israel
Museum, Jerusalem

pages 56-57
Fez Cabinet, 1997
Cibachrome
72 x 48 in. each, diptych
Courtesy of Patrick de
Brock, Belgium

page 58
Pillow B, 1994
Cibachrome
72 x 48 in.
Courtesy of a Private
Collection, Boston

page 59
Box and Stupa, 1994
Cibachrome
72 x 48 in.
Courtesy of Cent 8,
Paris

pages 60-61 and 101
Window & Bed (from
Windows from a Clear),
1997
Cibachrome
72 x 48 in. each, diptych
Courtesy of a Private
Collection, New York

pages 62-63
Lamp, Cabinet and table
(from *Chez P.S.*), 2000
Cibachrome
72 x 48 in. each
Collection of the artist

pages 64-65
English Tree (from
*Thèatre des Champs-
Elysèes*), 1996
Cibachrome
72 x 48 in. each, diptych
Courtesy of a Private
Collection, New York

page 66
Lake Towers-S (from
Chicago Series), 1995
Cibachrome
72 x 48 in.
Courtesy of Cent 8,
Paris

page 67
Glass with Hat, 1996
Cibachrome
72 x 48 in.
Courtesy of a Private
Collection, Switzerland

pages 68 and 99
Heart Pitcher (from
Annexed Things), 1997
Cibachrome
72 x 48 in.
Courtesy of a Private
Collection, Boston

page 71 left
Untitled (Portable
Room), 1986
Watercolor on cardboard
6 x 9 1/4 x 9 1/4 in.
Collection of the artist

page 71 right
*Drawing from Portable
Homes Series*, 1986
Watercolor
7 1/4 x 9 1/2 in.
Collection of the Artist

page 73
Several Dots, 1994
(from *Pergamon Series
Dark*)
Cibachrome
72 x 48 in.
Courtesy of Cent 8,
Paris

page 74
Lamp & Photos, 1994
Cibachrome
72 x 48 in. each, diptych
Courtesy of Barbara
Krakow, Boston

Seton Smith Photographs: Sensuous and Subtle Suggestions

by David Pagel

Not so long ago, people used the phrase "lost in thought" more frequently than we do now. It described what happened when someone stopped interacting with his or her surroundings in an active manner and appeared to drift off into a mysterious world that seemed to be considerably more captivating than the one in which the rest of us were left. Today, we tend to describe individuals who have such experiences as being "spaced out." It's not a complimentary term. Staring off into space with a blank face rarely impresses other people with one's capacity for complex thought or deep feeling. More often than not, it connotes failure, disengagement and a frustrating inability to focus on the task at hand. The fast-paced, image-saturated world in which we now live puts a higher priority on the constant, stay-in-touch connections made possible by cell phones—and the get-it-done-all-at-once simultaneity of multi-tasking—than it does on the seemingly inefficient stillness of reverie. Whether or not these developments lead to diminished attention spans, they make it more difficult for anyone to have enough time—or space—to get lost in thought.

Seton Smith's out-of-focus photographs make a space—and a time—for just this activity. For the past two decades, the Paris-based artist has been making works of supple beauty, calm allure and evocative silence. At one level, her sensuous images of recognizable objects invite viewers to daydream, to engage in reveries that drift freely from topic to topic without being burdened by logic or realism. Considerable pleasures are to be found when one momentarily escapes the goal-oriented, hand-to-mouth behavior that drives much of modern life. But these satisfactions only scratch the surface of Smith's multi-layered works. Her intriguing images also invite viewers to lose themselves in thought—to follow the progress of an idea as it slowly unfolds,

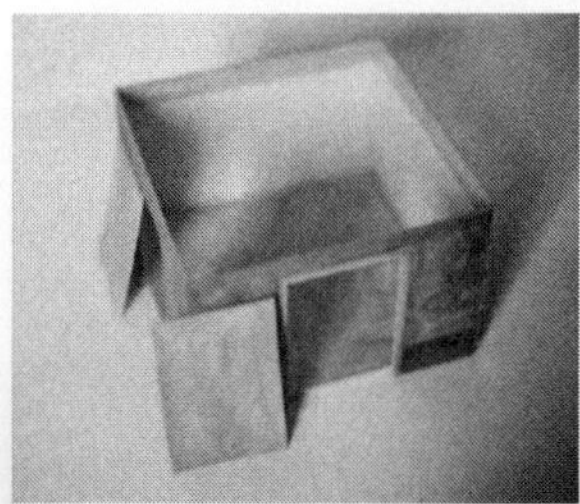 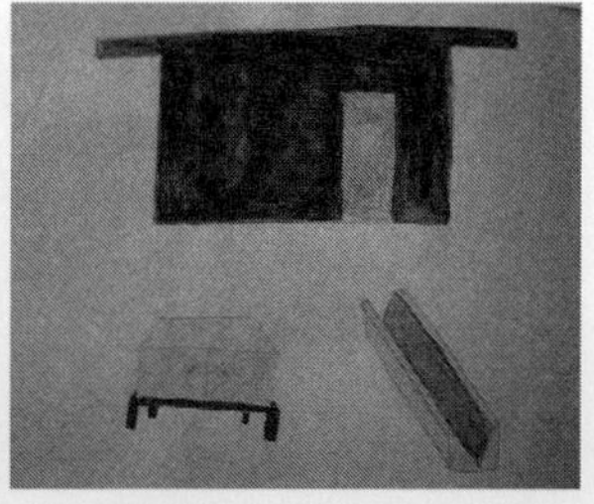

SETON SMITH
LEFT, *UNTITLED* (PORTABLE ROOM), 1986
RIGHT, *DRAWING FROM PORTABLE HOMES SERIES*, 1986

gradually branching out to include unanticipated connections to the rest of the world. By transforming the everyday experience of spaced-out inattentiveness into a point of departure for expansive flights of fancy, her works encourage sustained self-reflection and philosophic contemplation.

Rather than representing specific ideas, which can be clearly summarized, Smith's elusive art stimulates the *activity* of thinking—the intangible, impossible-to-picture process of pursuing an idea as it slips out of our grasp and compels us to keep reaching. It's a delicate operation, and she handles it masterfully. Instead of dazzling us with spectacular images that are supposed to be unforgettable, she presents seemingly offhand pictures of well-designed interiors and tasteful exteriors that set the stage for *experiences* that resonate in the mind's eye long afterward. Her photographs are memorable in the deep sense of the term. Like memories that keep changing as more time intervenes between the moment that created them and their recollection in the present, her works are attuned to the subjective nature of our interior lives. In them, thoughts and emotions swirl around one another endlessly.

No people appear in any of Smith's casually composed pictures. This leaves us free to feel that the places she depicts exist for us alone. Of course that's an illusion, but it's not one animated by delusions of grandeur or overweening narcissism. There's nothing exclusive, elitist or egomaniacal about the rooms and landscapes Smith invites us to visit (in our imaginations). Although rare and precious objects regularly appear in her photographs and installations—including ancient Greek vases, a huge Japanese bronze bell and ornate staircases that once belonged to European aristo-crats—they never give the impression of being behind-the-scenes peeks into the private lives of privileged insiders or up-close and personal views of exotic collectibles. Snob appeal plays no part in Smith's wonderfully humble works. Open and available to anyone with an imagination, her oeuvre embraces an ethos of democratic accessibility—of discovering, in common things, experiences of uncommon power.

All of the objects in Smith's dreamy images from the mid-1980s to the late 1990s are displayed in public institutions or on their grounds. Visiting archaeological museums, temples and chateaus that are no longer privately owned but are part of the public trust, she is as likely to photograph a lighting fixture as she is to aim her camera at the ancient statues and architectural ruins it is meant to illuminate. Vitrines, cabinets, display cases, and roped-off rooms appear with greater frequency than the historical artifacts and priceless items they contain. In many photographs, sensuous sunlight streams through scrim-covered windows, bathing empty spaces in a warm glow or casting cool shadows that add even more mystery. In other images, she records and accentuates the ghostly reflections of objects and their surroundings captured in protective glass covers.

Smith doesn't lavish attention on seemingly incidental details to elevate them to the status of high art. Nor does she level a conventional institutional critique of the means and methods of presentation that mediate a viewer's experience of the objects themselves. Instead, her photographs capture the atmosphere of museums, the sense that when you walk through the front door you enter a world in which the hustle and bustle of everyday life has been muffled and time's passage has wound down to a slow crawl. Even when Smith visits major institutions, such as the Pergamon Museum in Berlin, she makes photographs that look as if the objects in them belong in small,

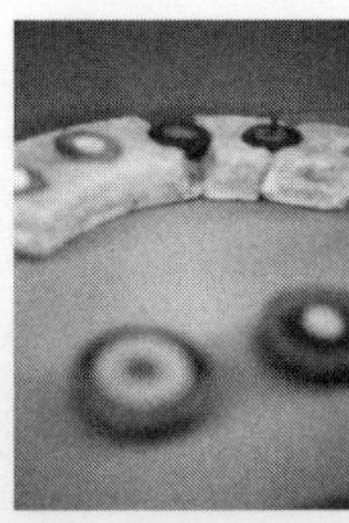

SETON SMITH
SEVERAL DOTS (FROM *PERGAMON SERIES DARK*), 1994

off-the-beaten-track venues, ones that never host blockbuster exhibitions, rarely draw more than a handful of visitors on a winter afternoon, and usually feature pieces that are respectable but hardly exemplary. The timeless perfection of masterpieces is a myth her pictures play no part in perpetuating. The same goes for the pomp and ceremony that often accompany the display of such symbols of eternal genius. At once discreet and wistful, her charmingly romantic works embody a type of temporality that is suffused with bittersweet poignancy and the knowledge that everything is vulnerable to change.

Nearly all of Smith's photographs, including recent images of parks, gardens, urban courtyards and the interiors of apartments, have the fleeting presence of things glimpsed out of the corner of one's eye. This gives them the surreptitious, even fugitive quality of moments stolen from a day's busy schedule—unpredictable instants when our minds drift away from what we are supposed to be concentrating on and go nowhere in particular. In such moods, thoughts often come to us, as if by accident and despite our best efforts. Something similar happens before Smith's enchanting photographs, which prefer the intimacy of subtle suggestions to the clarity of direct statements.

David Pagel is a Los Angeles-based critic and curator who regularly contributes to the *Los Angeles Times* as well as many international art publications.

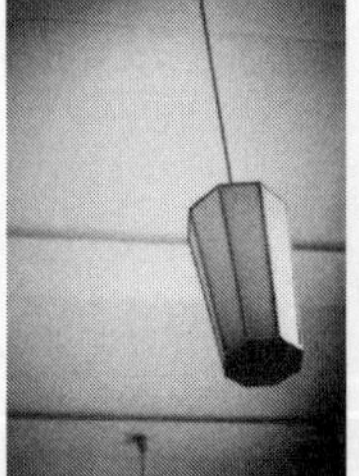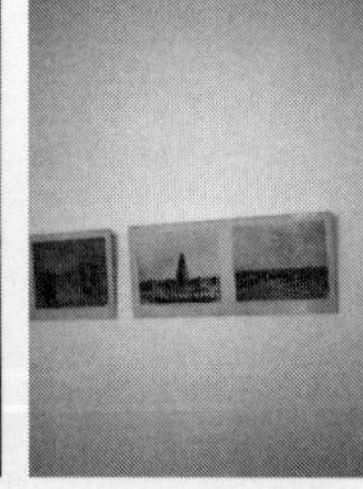

SETON SMITH
LAMP & PHOTOS, 1994

Knowing Through the Body: The Art of Kiki Smith
by Eleanor Heartney

When she was an aspiring young artist, Kiki Smith recalls, her father, the sculptor Tony Smith, gave her a box of cylinders, cones and cubes to draw. When she could not get the hang of perspective, he wisely advised her, "Don't draw what you see, draw what you know."

That advice runs through the art works she has made ever since. What does Smith know? She knows the body, or more precisely, she knows through the body. She rejects the Western world's long-standing tendencies to privilege vision over the other senses and to charge artists with the task of creating an objective representation of the visible realm. Instead, she works from the inside out, expressing a corporeal sense of reality in which taste, touch and smell are as important as sight. For Smith, knowledge is subjective and cannot be separated from the sensate experience of the world. This is, she believes, a particularly female way of understanding reality. As she once told an interviewer, "women don't separate their identity of self from their identity of themselves as bodies."

Thus, from one perspective, Smith's work is the quintessential expression of the stereotypical "feminine" sensibility. Deeply concerned with issues of beauty and decoration, she employs materials traditionally associated with women's crafts—glass, paper, wax, fabric and lace, along with more "masculine" substances like bronze and pewter. Her subjects often seem to hail from the realm of what she calls "girlie" art— among them lace doilies, the human body, glass stars and birds.

However, it is immediately apparent to any astute viewer of her work that something has gone seriously awry. The birds are scattered over the ground, dead of some mysterious disease. The doilies double as human cells or bodily orifices. The glass

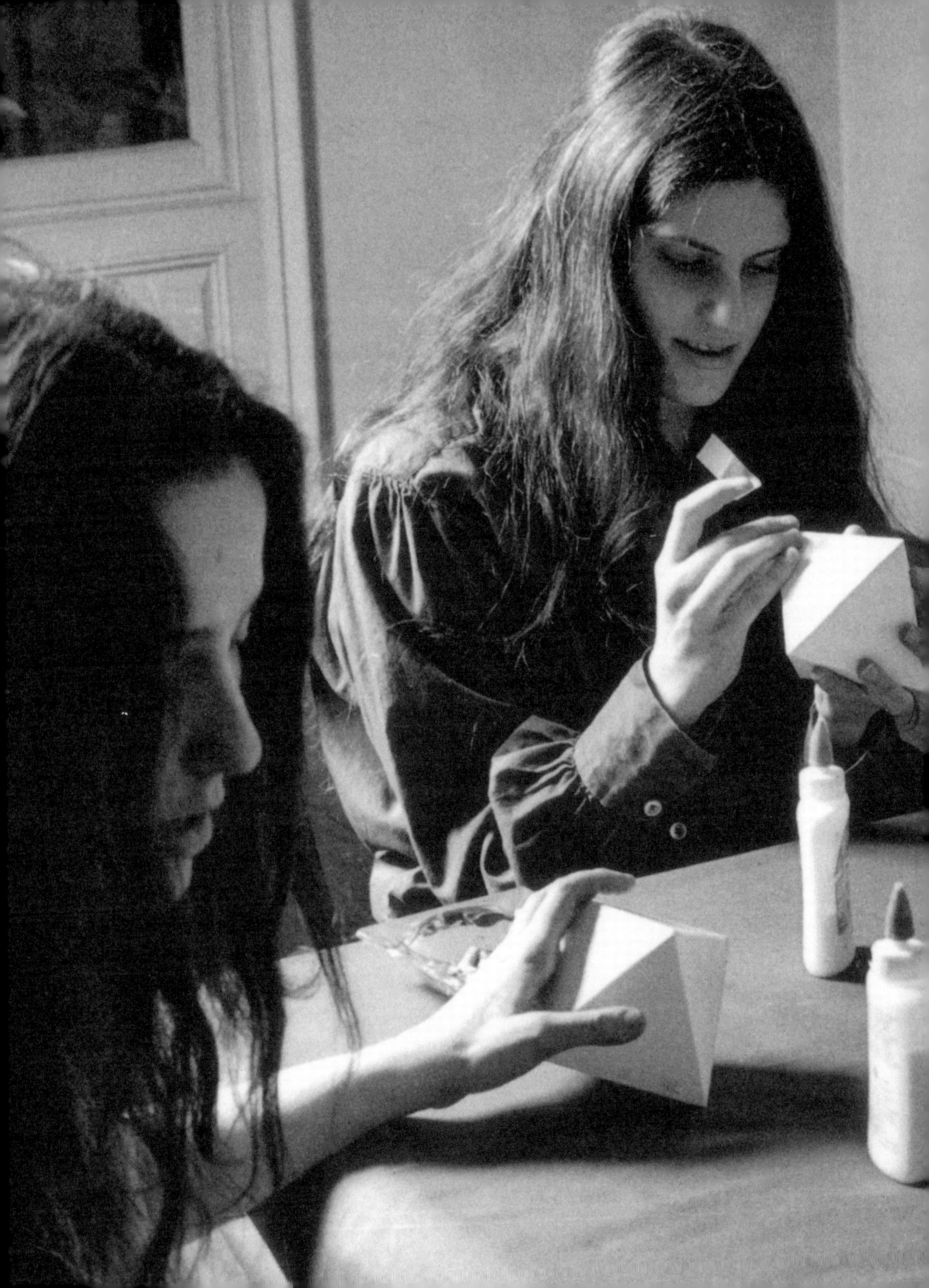

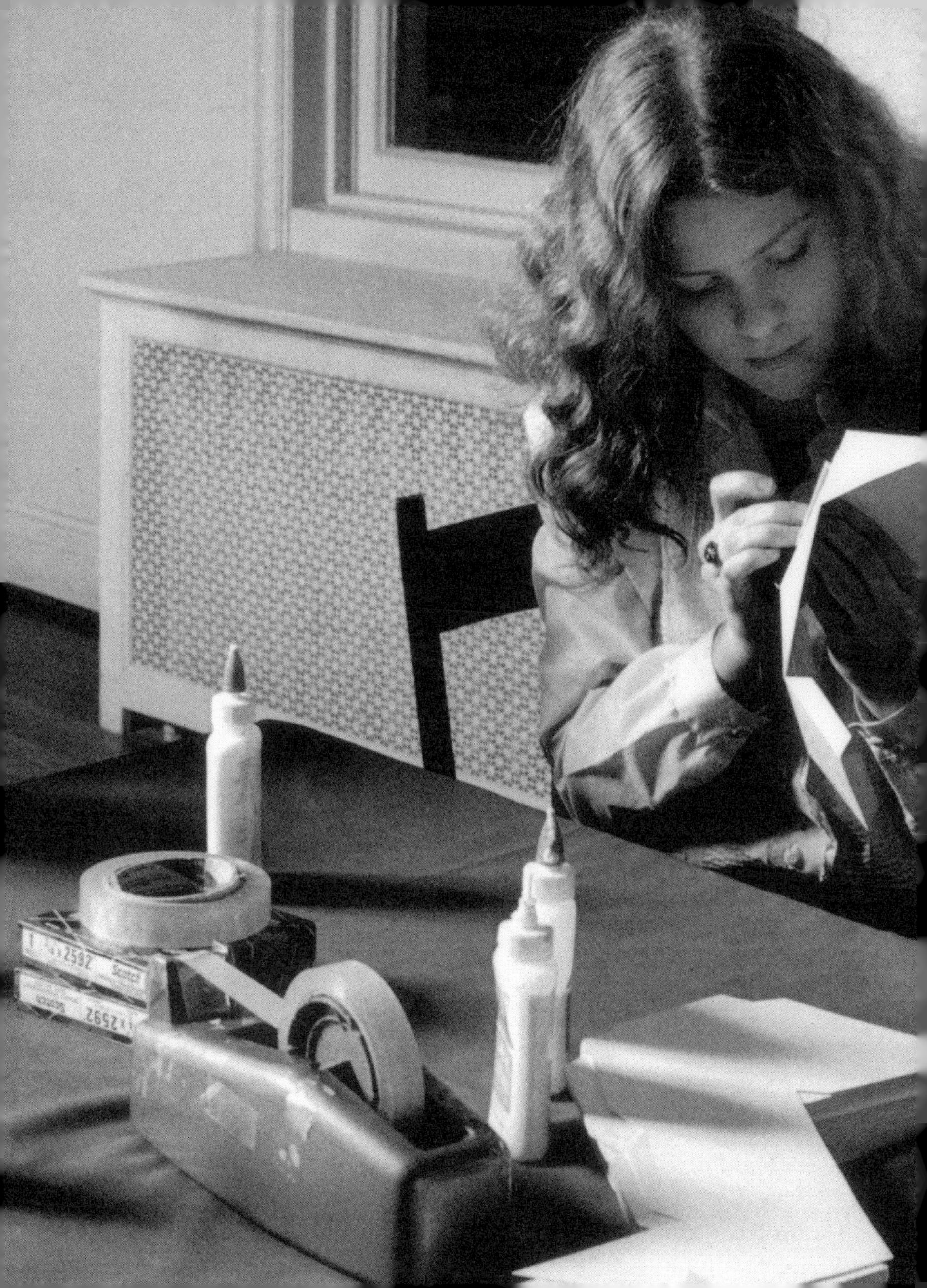

stars lie on the ground next to sculpted animal scat. The nudes lean against the wall with patterned fabric intestines spilling from their bellies or they dangle in midair with breast milk, blood or semen running down their legs.

Smith's work presents a strange mix of seduction, elegance, disgust and vulnerability. Though she draws on the venerable tradition of the nude, her sculptures based on the human body directly challenge the revulsion that many contemporary Americans feel toward the body and its processes. Her first full-scale body sculptures, completed in 1990, present a naked man and woman fashioned from beeswax. Their bodies sag as they leak body fluids. She describes them in tragic terms, noting that these works are about "being psychologically thwarted. Her milk nourishes nothing, and his semen propagates nothing. It is about having all this potential life and yet having no life."

Later she created a series of figures that deal directly with body fluids and excretions. These include life-size figures with yellow glass urine or red glass menstrual blood trailing from their bodies. Particularly unsettling is *Tale*, which consists of a naked female figure on all fours excreting a long trail of feces. Such works are meant to embody psychological conditions—the feeling of loss of control or of being unable to escape one's mental baggage.

For Smith, the body serves as a means of understanding our place in the world. For many years it was her principal subject. Working in a variety of mediums such as glass, paper, wax, and bronze and encompassing sculpture, installation, drawings and prints, she has long been preoccupied with the beauty of the purely physical aspects of the human body. She has created exquisite glass stomachs and sperm, red stained

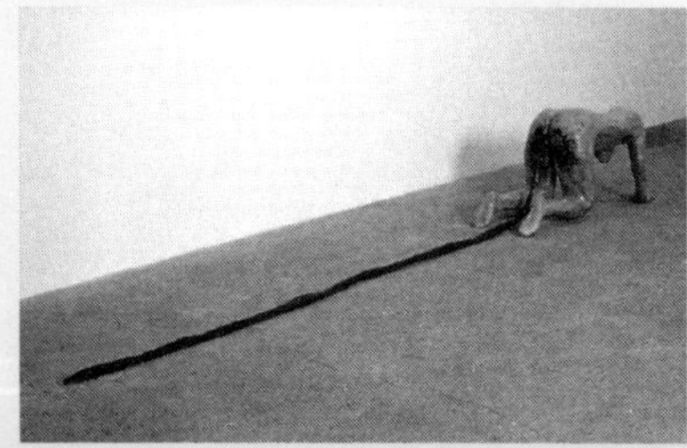

KIKI SMITH
TALE, 1992

paper skin and rolled-paper umbilical cords, terra-cotta rib cages, ceramic hearts and bronze uteruses.

Her early work included re-creations of internal organs and systems, including sculpted versions of the stomach, bladder, liver, heart and brain created from fragile and potentially ephemeral materials. Explorations of birth imagery like wombs were followed by evocations of body fluids and internal organs. Next came representations of skin and muscles and finally, the entire human body. Recently she has continued this outward trajectory, turning to landscape and fairy tales in works that retain the unsettling paradoxes of her body sculptures.

She describes her evolution thus: "For three years my work was about birth. Then for four years it was about fluids, the body and the nervous system. My work has evolved from minute particles within the body up through the body and landed outside the body. In the last few years it's been inside and outside. Now I want to roam around in the landscape."

Not surprisingly, this is a landscape experienced from the inside out. When animals—deer, birds, wolves and butterflies—appear, it is clear that there is no comfortable division between the human and natural worlds. Smith's animals are avatars of primitive forces to which humans are equally heir. Sometimes there is no distinction between the human and nonhuman world, as when Smith depicts Mary Magdalene naked and covered with hair, nearly metamorphosing into a wild beast, or the Greek nymph Daphne in the process of turning into a tree. In Smith's world, even stars, trees and stones are anthropomorphized and exude a mysterious life spirit.

Recently Smith has been delving into the dark side of fairy tales, which, as Bruno

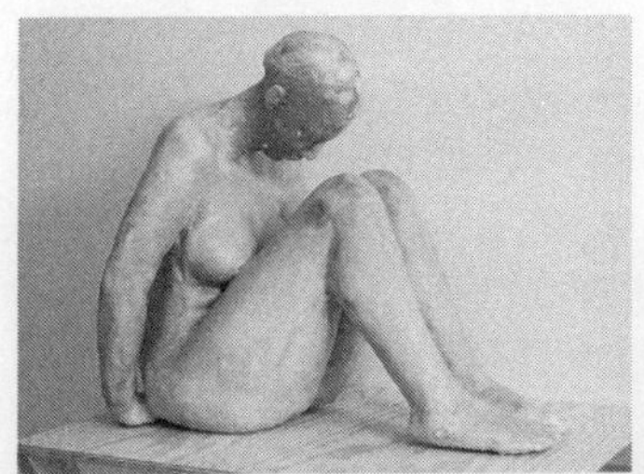 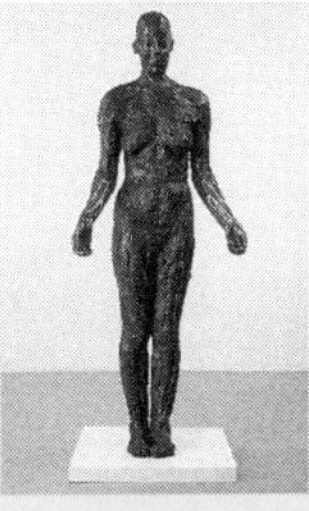

KIKI SMITH
LEFT, *UNTITLED*, 1992
RIGHT, *VIRGIN MARY*, 1994

Bettelheim has told us, often provide children and adults with a cathartic release of primitive fears and psychological traumas. Far from the Disneyfied whitewashes of popular children's cartoons, Smith goes back to the violent sources of these ancient tales. Her Red Riding Hood, for instance, is at once a vulnerable little girl and the embodiment of savage impulses. At one point she actually melds with the wolf, revealing an essential similarity between victim and prey.

The idea of knowledge through the body runs counter to powerful forces in contemporary American culture. It challenges the rationalist view that holds evidence of the eye to be the bedrock of verifiable knowledge. But seeing is not always believing. Body knowledge privileges aspects of experience that are subjective, visceral and hidden from view. In part, Smith's embrace of this principle reflects her experience as a woman in a world where female perspectives are often dismissed as "emotional," "personal" and "irrational." It also stems from her early immersion in Catholicism, which emphasizes the intermingling of body and soul. As Smith notes, in her work "spiritual dilemmas are being played out physically. That puts me in a Catholic tradition...."

Kiki Smith brings us back into contact with aspects of life that contemporary society tends to suppress. The power of her work is to remind us that by looking beneath the surface, we discover that we are composed of flesh and blood and bone, and that we are beset with desires and dreams and fears that simple rationality can never comprehend.

Eleanor Heartney is a New York-based art writer, cultural critic and Contributing Editor to *Art in America* and *Artpress*.

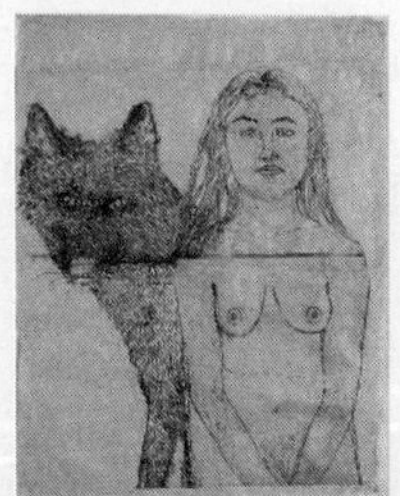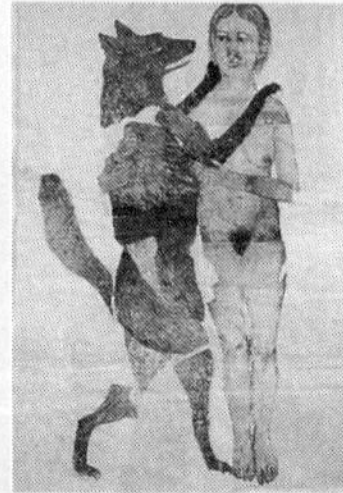

KIKI SMITH
LEFT, *UNTITLED*, 1999
RIGHT, *SAINTE GENEVIÈVE*, 1999

SMITH
KIKI
SMITH

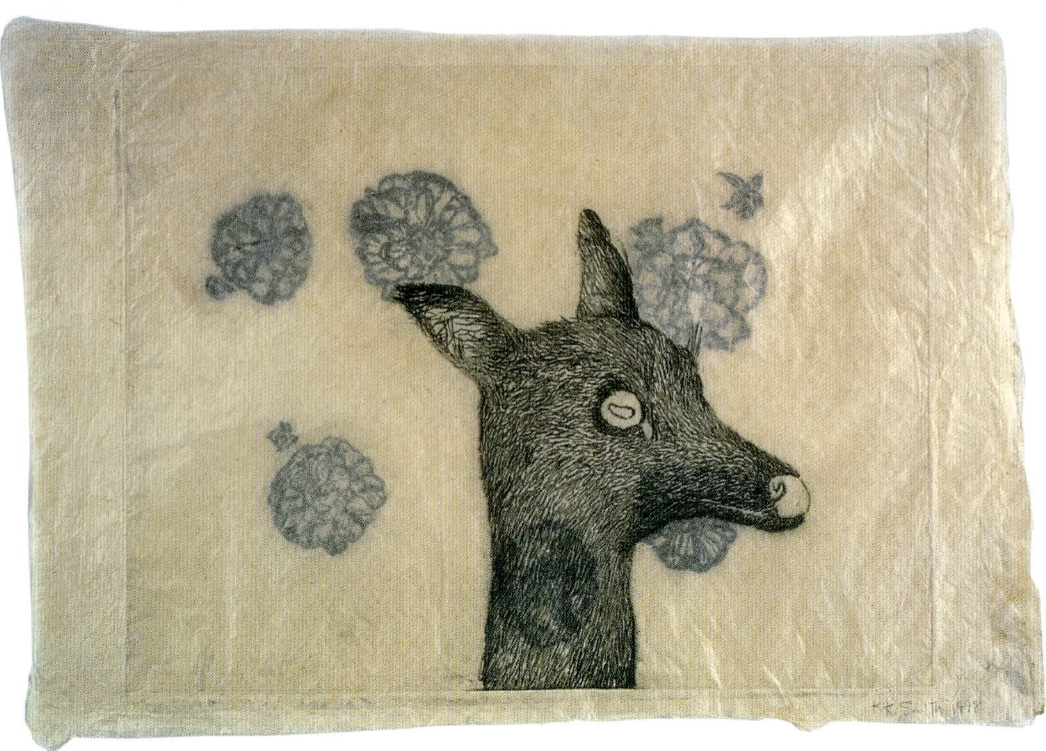

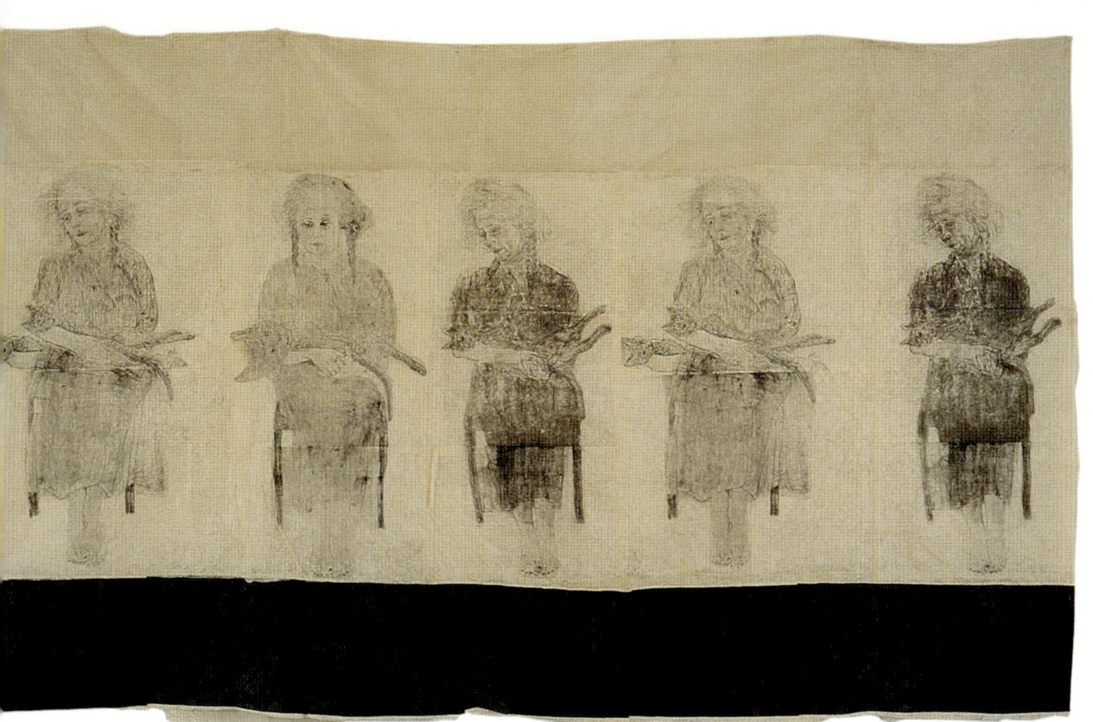

84/85

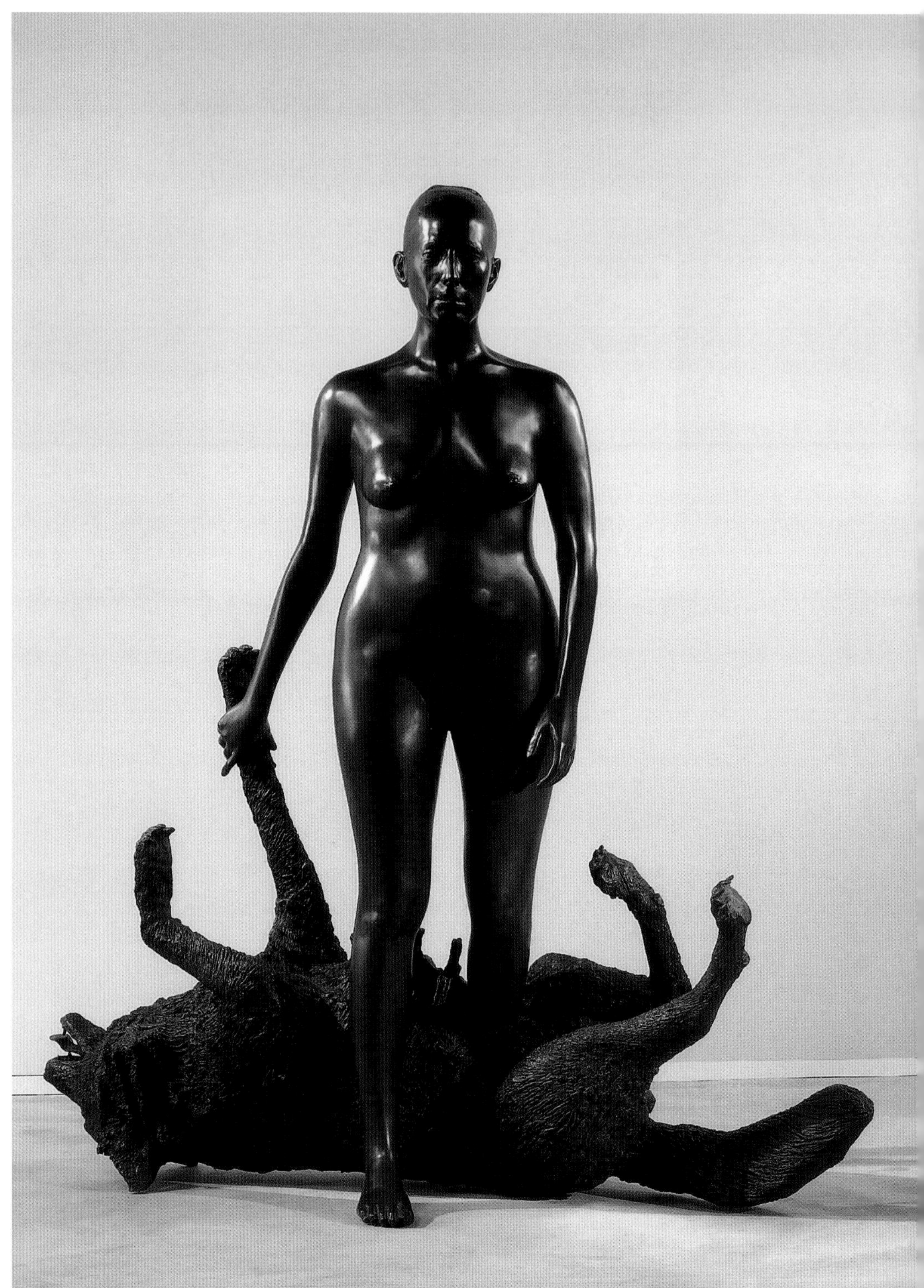

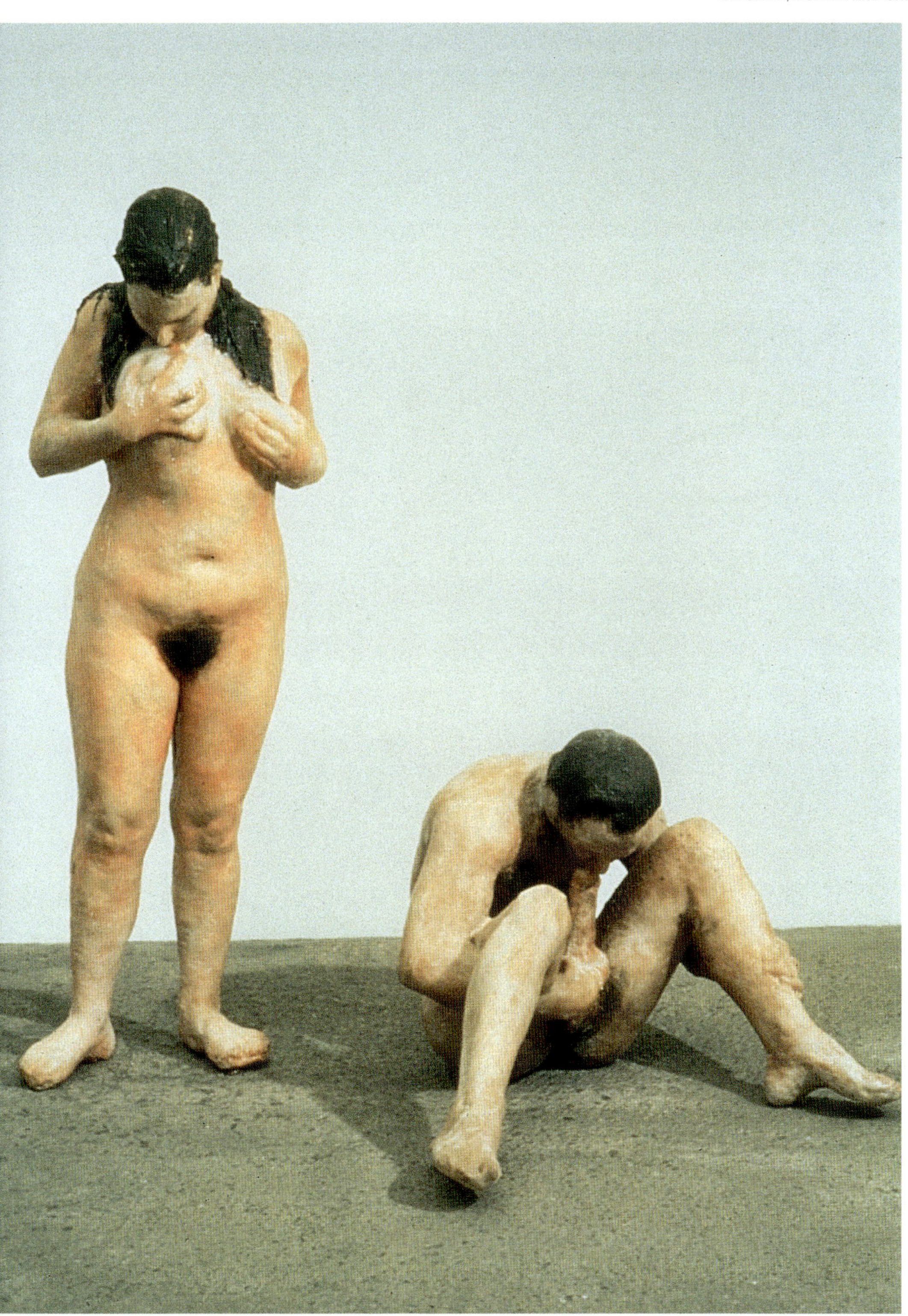

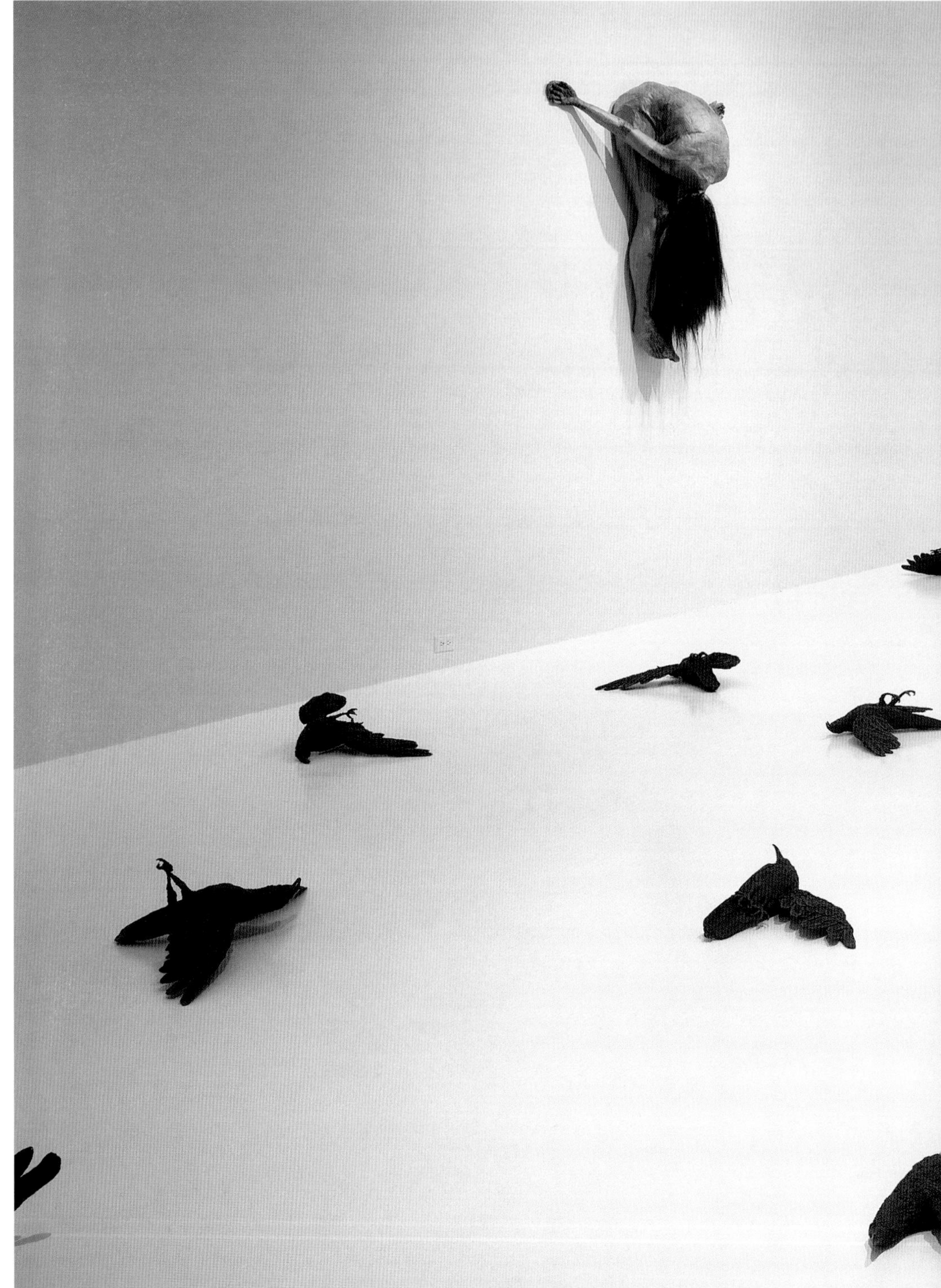

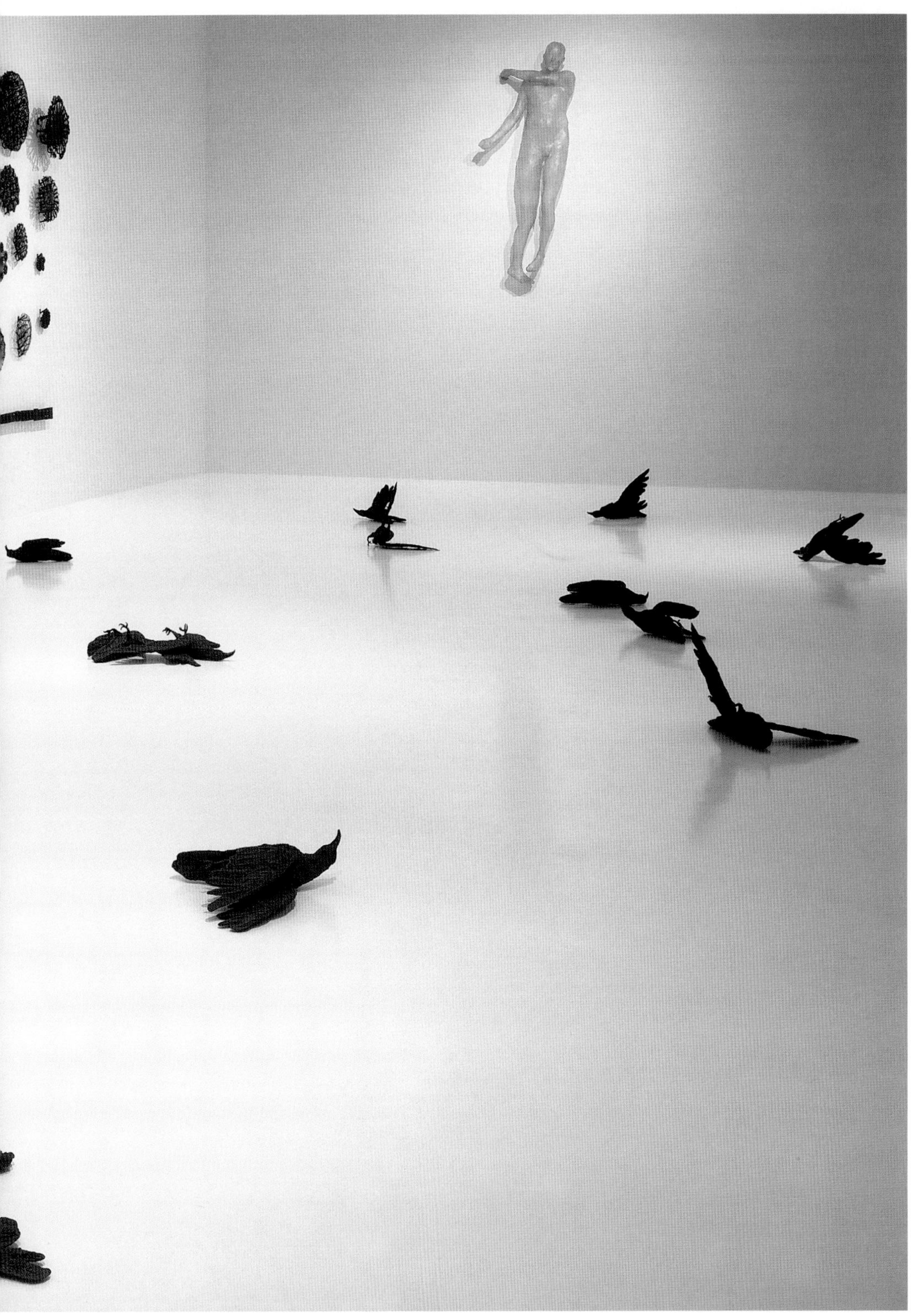

KIKI SMITH, JERSEY CROWS, 1995

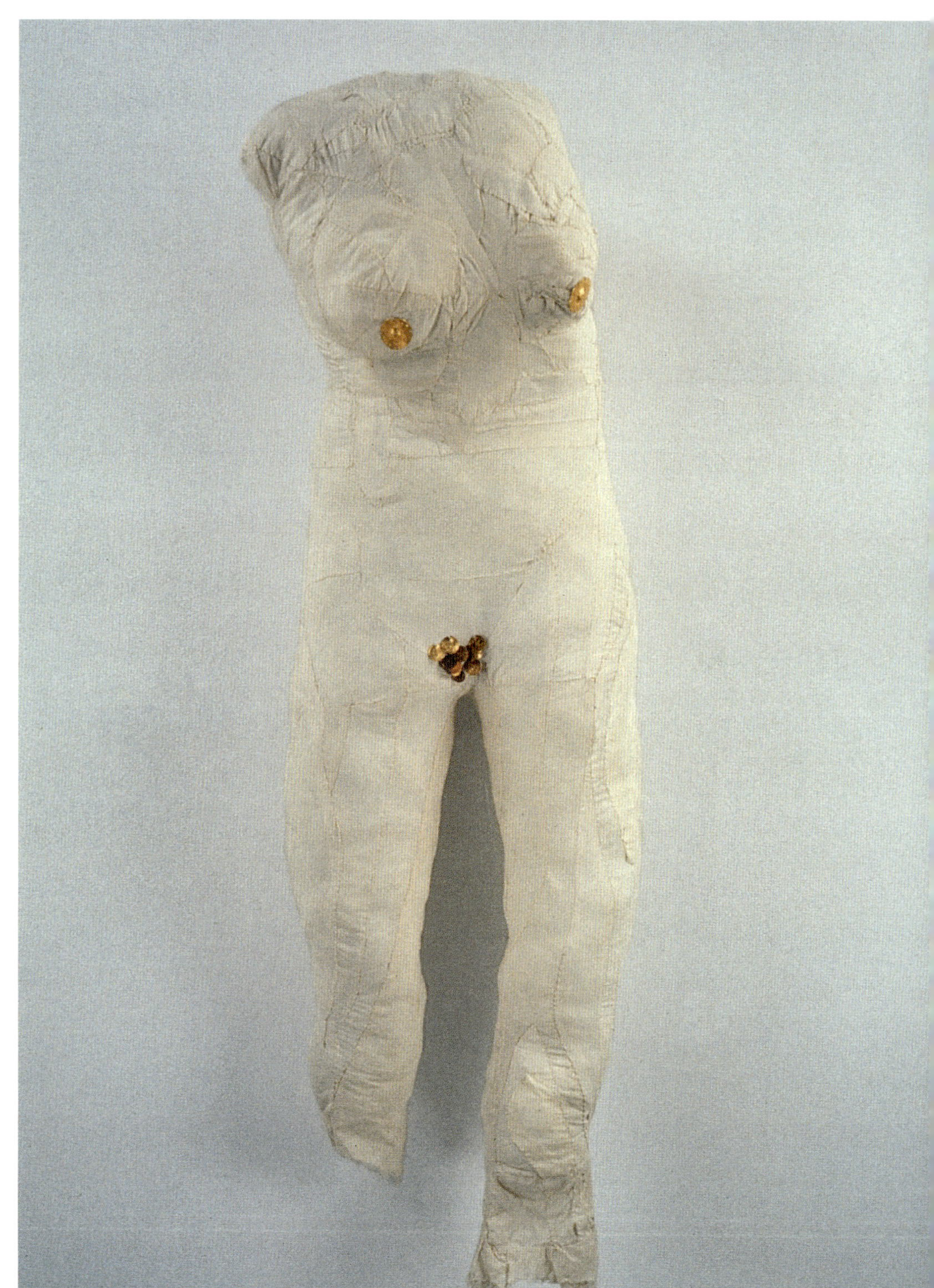

88/89

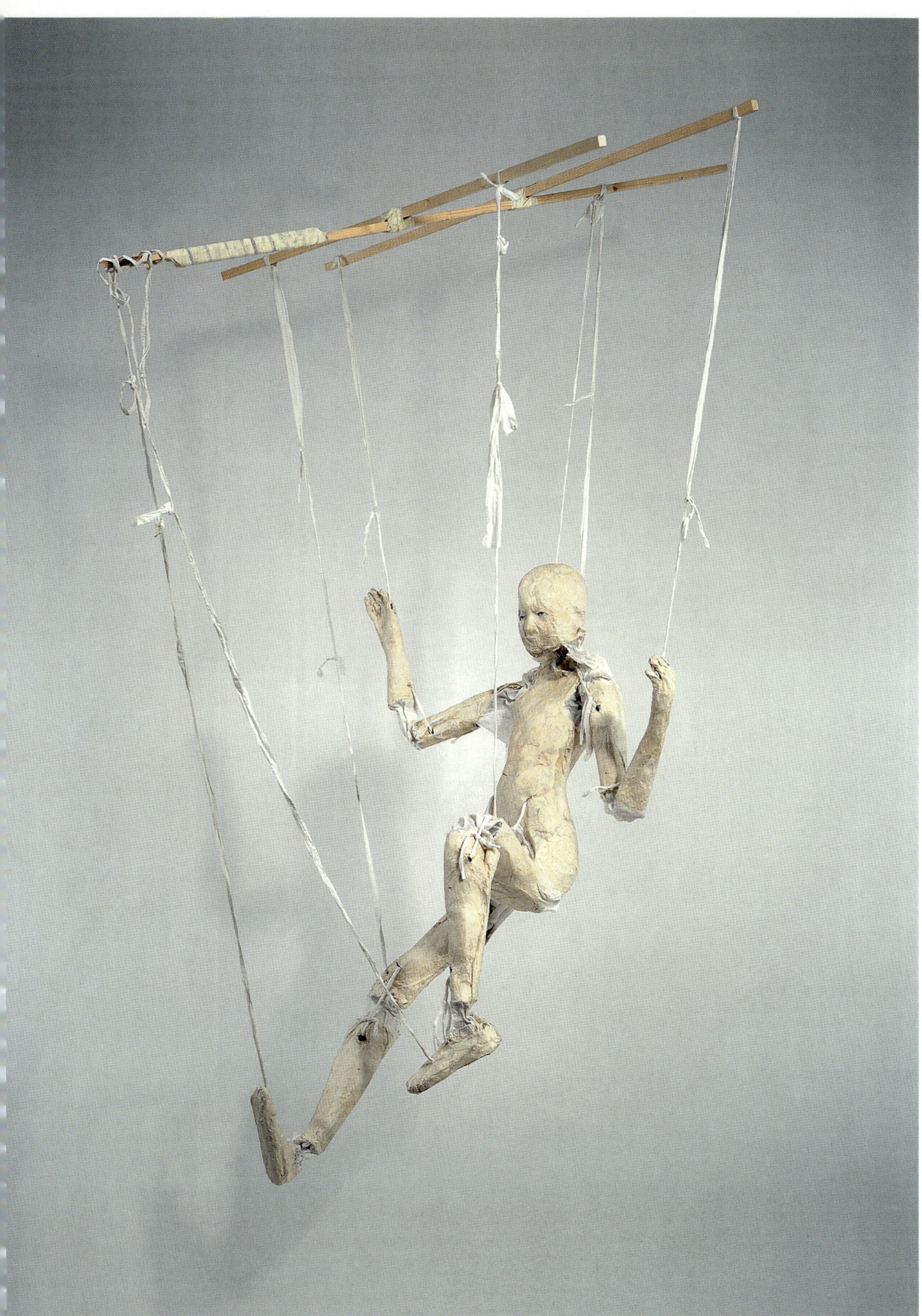

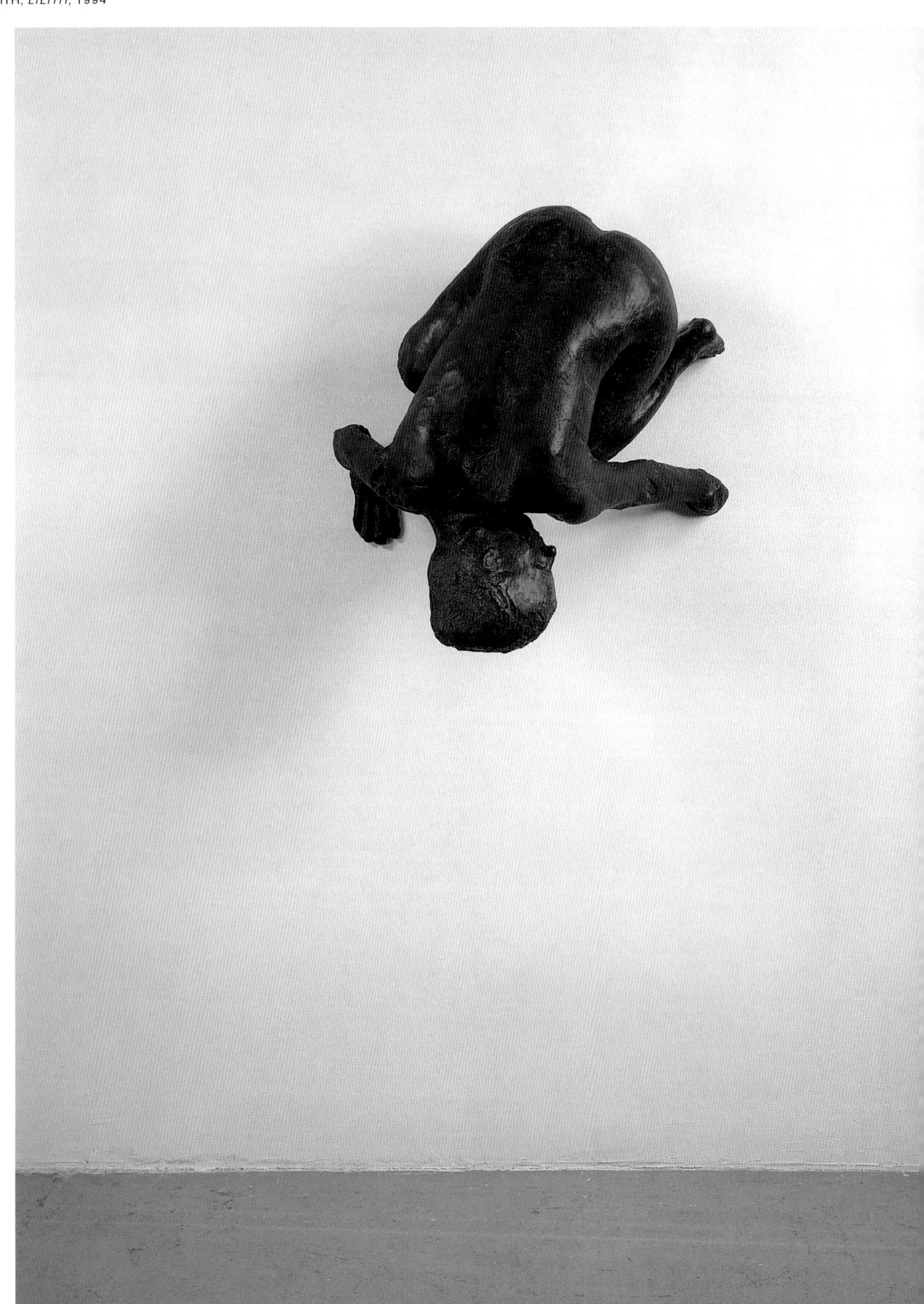

90/91

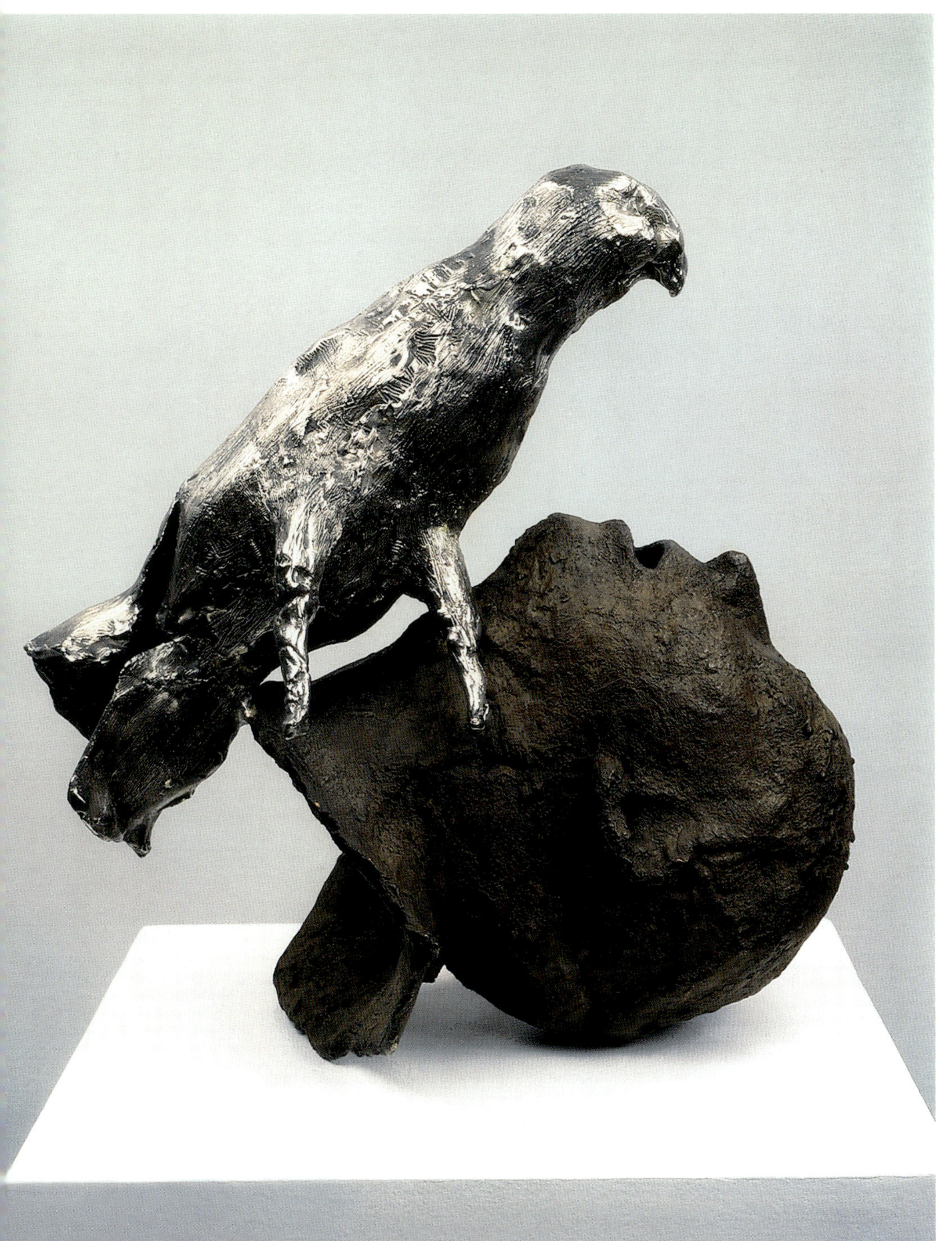

KIKI SMITH, *HEAD WITH BIRD I*, 1994

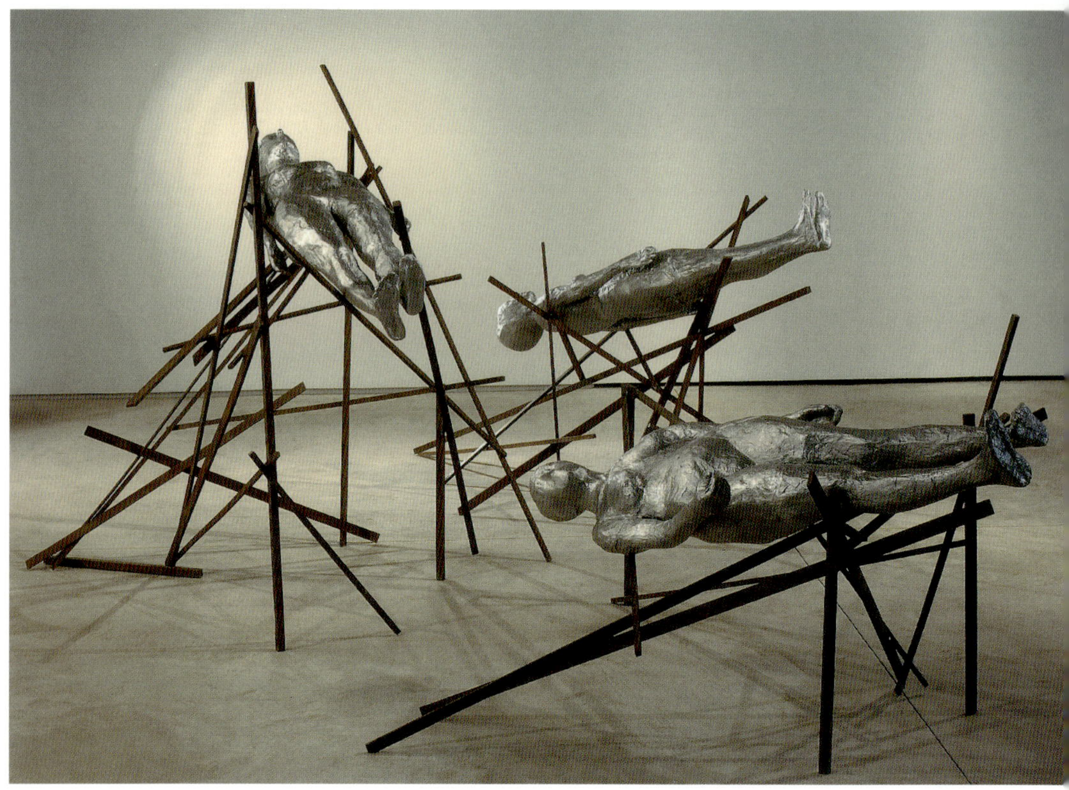

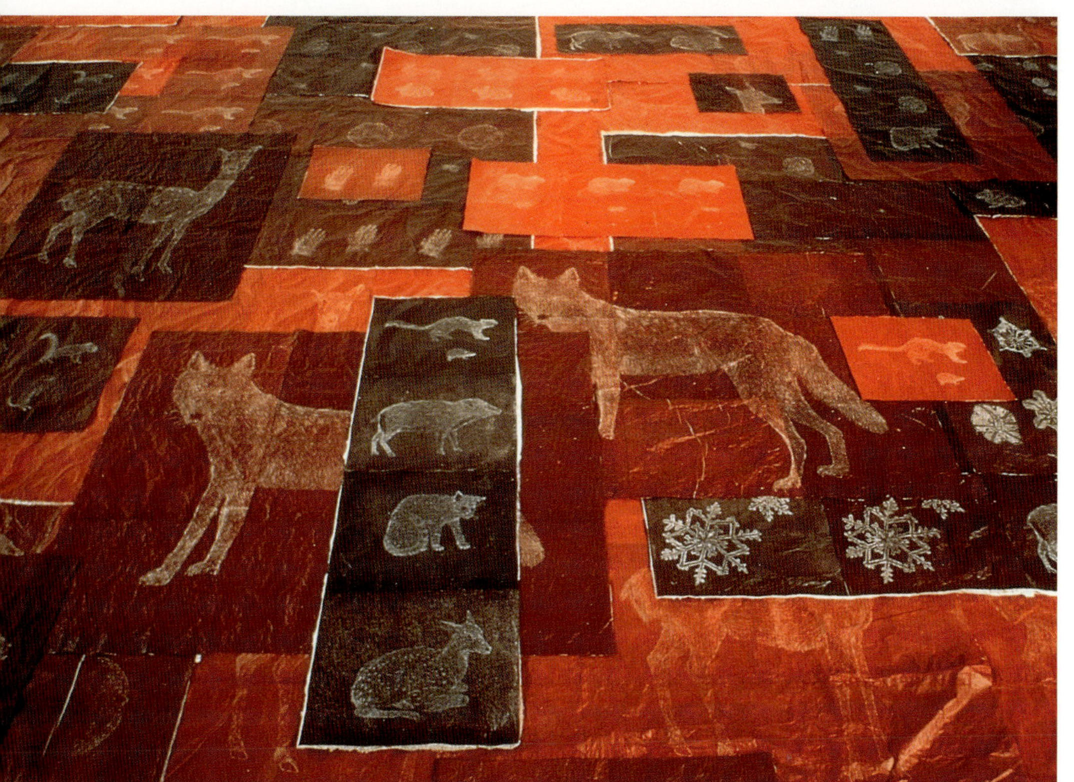

KIKI SMITH, *PEABODY (ANIMAL DRAWINGS)*, 1996

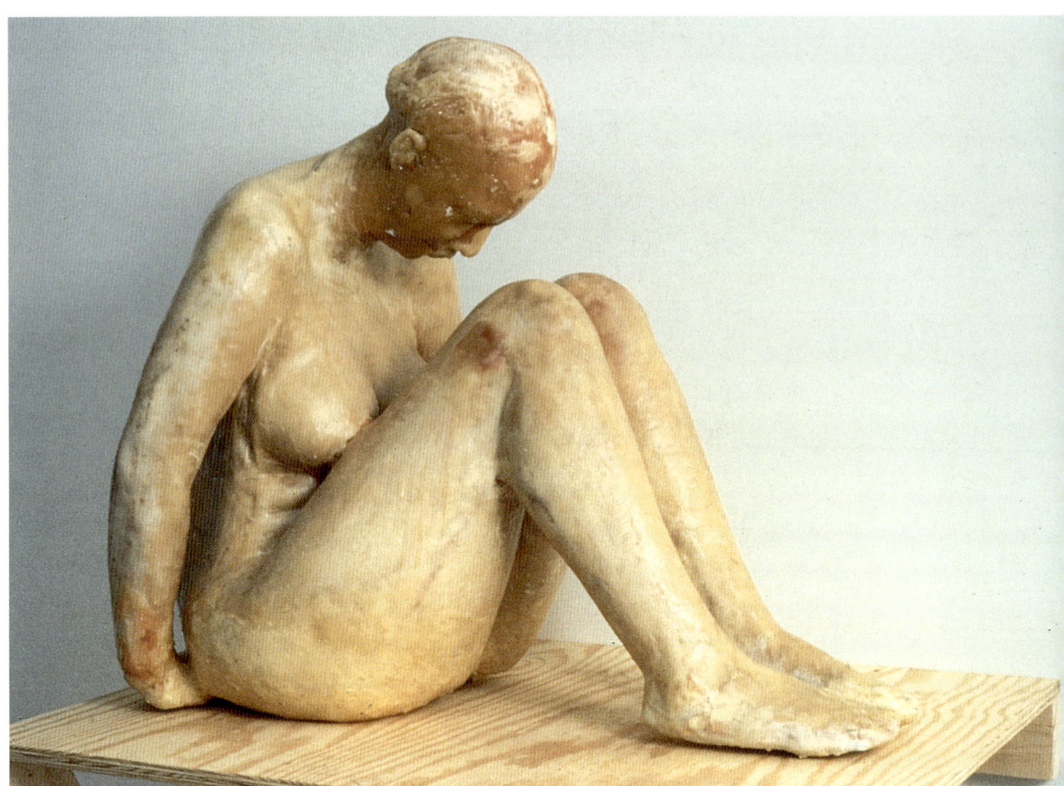

94/95

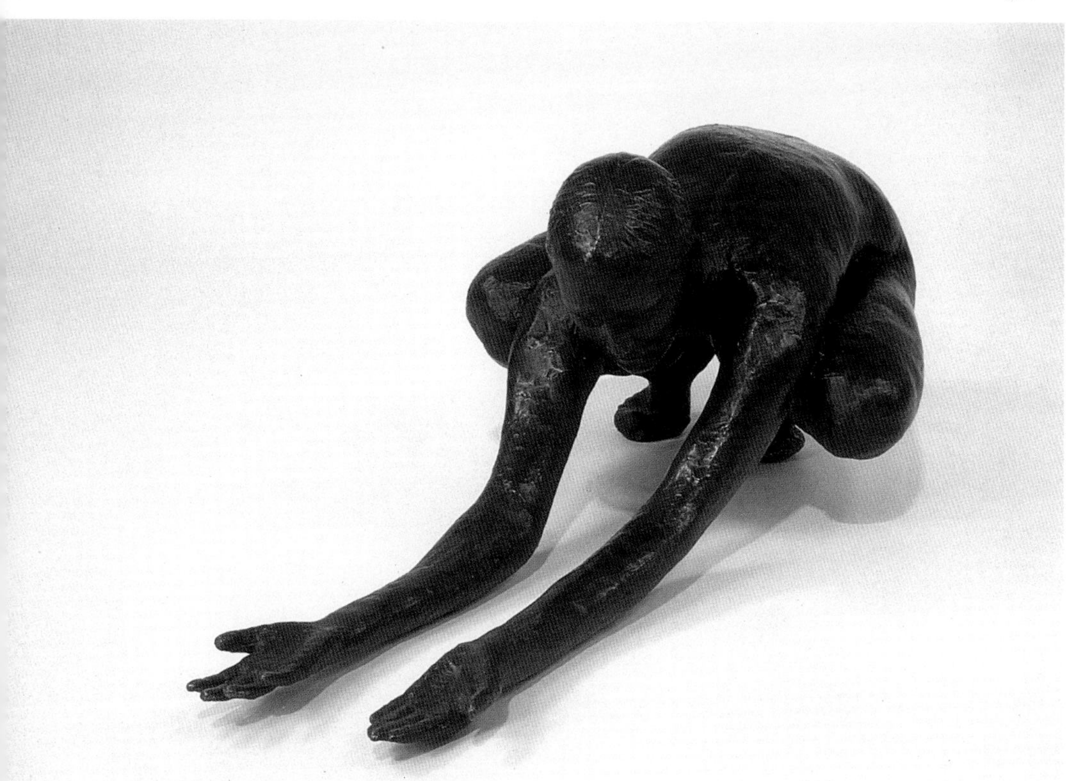

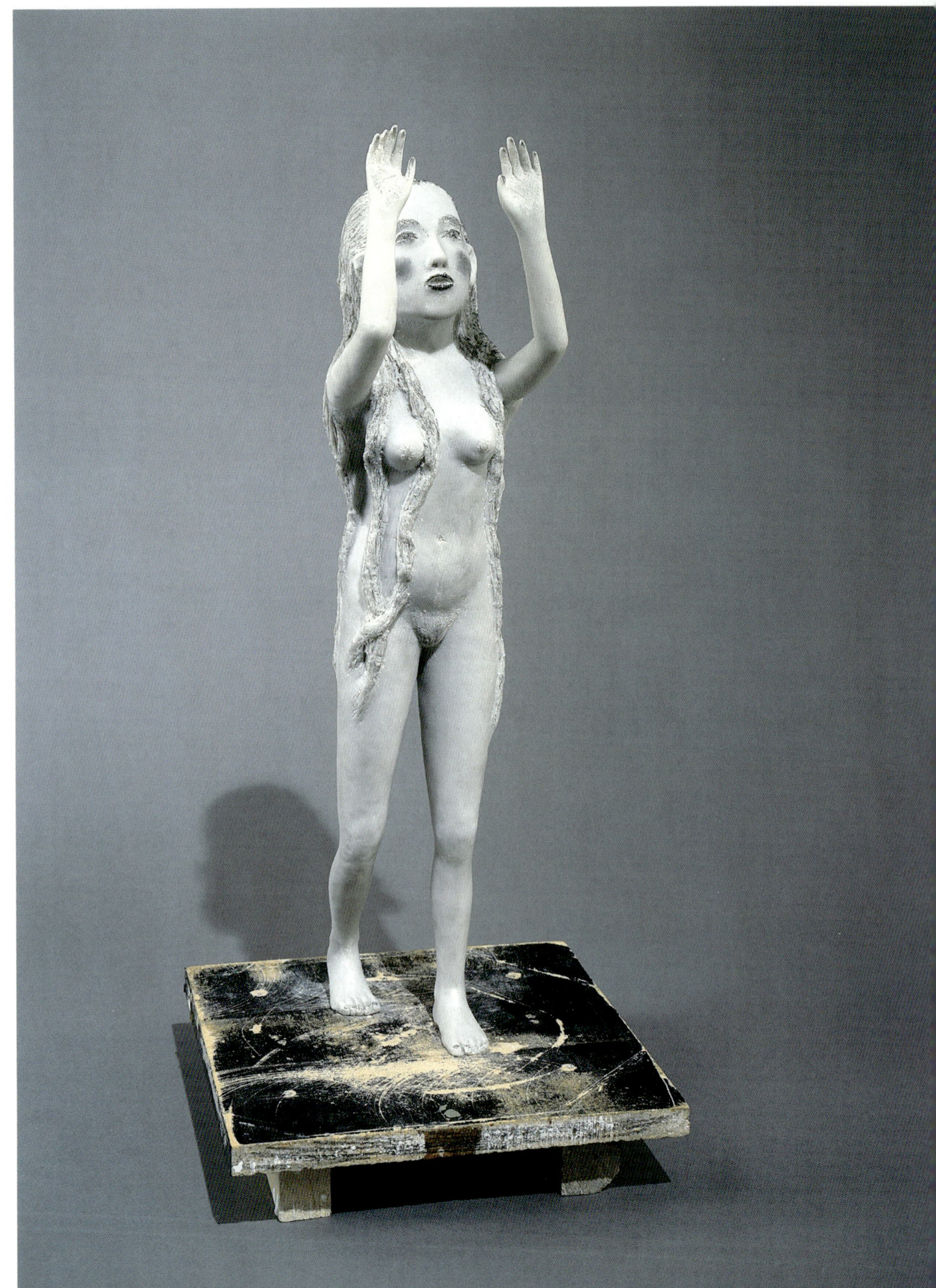

96/97

Plate List
Kiki Smith

All artworks © Kiki Smith

page 49
Untitled (Sperm),
1989-90
Lead crystal
Dimensions variable
Detail Image
Collection of The
Museum of Contempo-
rary Art, Los Angeles
Gift of Lannan Foundation

page 78
Tale, 1992
Wax, pigment, papier-
mâché
160 x 23 x 23 in.
Photograph courtesy
of the artist
Collection of Jeffrey
Deitch, New York

**pages 79 left small
image and 94**
Untitled, 1992
Wax, cheesecloth, wood
and dye
28 x 36 x 24 in.
Collection of Emily
Fisher Landau, New York

**page 79 right small
image**
Virgin Mary, 1994
Phosphorous bronze
and silver
66 x 25 1/2 x 17 in.
Ed. of 3 + 1 AP
Photograph by Sarah
Harper Gifford, courtesy
PaceWildenstein
Private Collection

page 80 left
Untitled, 1999
Ink on paper
36 1/2 x 30 1/4 in.
Photograph by Ellen
Page Wilson, courtesy
PaceWildenstein
Private collection

page 80 right
Sainte Geneviève, 1999
Ink on Nepal paper
74 1/8 x 51 1/2 in.
Photograph by Gordon
Riley Christmas,
courtesy
PaceWildenstein
Private collection

page 82
Double Animals, 1998
Ink on paper with collage
and methyl cellulose
20 x 30 in.
Photograph by Gordon
Riley Christmas, courtesy
PaceWildenstein
Private collection

page 83
Pietà, 1999
Ink on paper
92 x 151 1/2 in.
Photograph by Ellen
Page Wilson, courtesy
PaceWildenstein
Private collection

page 84
Rapture, 2001
Bronze, Ed. 2/3 + 1 AP
67 1/4 x 62 x 26 1/4 in.
Photograph by Ellen
Page Wilson, courtesy
PaceWildenstein
Collection of the artist

page 85
Mother and Child, 1993
Wax and pigment
Life size
Photograph courtesy
of the artist
Courtesy of the Dakis
Joannou Collection,
Athens

pages 86-87
Jersey Crows, 1995
Silicon bronze
27 units, 16 x 19 1/2 x
23 1/2 in. each, installation
dimensions variable
Photograph by Ellen
Page Wilson, courtesy
PaceWildenstein
Private collection

page 88
Body, 1995
Cotton, polyester fiber
fill, gold
61 x 18 1/2 x 14 3/4 in.
Photograph by Ellen
Page Wilson, courtesy
PaceWildenstein
Collection of the artist

page 89
Puppet, 2000
Nepal paper, muslin,
glass
54 x 15 x 9 3/4 in.
Photograph by Ellen
Page Wilson, courtesy
PaceWildenstein
Collection of the artist

page 90
Lilith, 1994
Bronze with glass eyes
33 x 27 1/2 x 19 in.
Unique, 1 in a series of 3
plus 1 unique AP
Photograph by Ellen
Page Wilson
The Metropolitan Museum
of Art, Purchase, Roy R.
and Marie S. Neuberger
Gift, 1996

page 91
Head with Bird I, 1994
(Side)
Phosphorous bronze
and white bronze
12 x 12 x 6 1/2 in
Photograph by Ellen
Page Wilson
Collection of Emily
Fisher Landau, New York

page 92
Moon on Crutches, 2002
Cast aluminum and
bronze
Fig. 1, 44 1/2 x 92 1/2 x 84
in.; Fig. 2, 74 1/2 x 68 x
83 1/2; Fig. 3, 54 x 109 1/2
x 67 in.
Installation dimensions
variable
Unique
Installation shot consist-
ing of three individual
works entitled *Moon on
Crutches*
Photograph by Ellen
Page Wilson, courtesy
PaceWildenstein

page 93
*Peabody (Animal
Drawings)*, 1996
Ink on paper
Detail
No longer extant in this
form
Photography courtesy of
the artist

page 95
Untitled, 1992
Bronze with patina
55 x 28 x 24 in.
Photograph courtesy
of the artist, Collection
of the artist

page 96
Eve, 2001
Manzini (resin & marble
dust) and graphite
20 3/8 x 5 x 6 3/4 in., AP 1
of 2, Ed. of 3 + 2 APs
Photograph by Ellen
Page Wilson, courtesy
PaceWildenstein
Collection of the artist

page 99
Born, 2002
Bronze
39 x 101 x 24 in.
Ed. 1/3 + 1 AP
Photograph Ellen Page
Wilson, courtesy
PaceWildenstein
Private collection

**page 102 left small
image**
*Uro-Genital System
(Female)*, 1986
Bronze
20 x 11 in.
Photograph courtesy
Anthony d'Offay Gallery,
London

**page 102 right small
image**
*Uro-Genital System
(Male)*, 1986
Bronze
20 x 11 in.
Photograph courtesy
Anthony d'Offay Gallery,
London

The Smiths: On the Edge of Dreams
by Michael Rush

In a 1967 cover story in *Time* magazine, Tony Smith was quoted as saying, "My own personal feeling is that all my sculpture is on the edge of dreams. They come close to the unconscious despite their geometry. On one level, my work has clarity. On another it is chaotic and imagined."[1]

There is no value in attempting to force-fit links among artists, even artists from the same family. On the face of it, Tony Smith's monumental, severe minimalist forms share little in common with Seton's ethereal photographs or Kiki's rough-hewn body parts. We should leave it to the poets to fabricate metaphors, or, in this case, similes, that can bind these three in a common pursuit. That said, it is natural even for the rest of us to venture below the surface, beneath apparent and real disparities in search of links among artists of different generations especially if they share the same blood. If Tony, minimalist master, can speak of dreams and the unconscious, we need not look too far into his daughters' work for affinities. For what is Kiki's bronze of a woman being born from the womb of a deer (*Born*, 2002) if not a dreamscape frozen in time, and what is Seton's *Heart Pitcher*, 1997, an ancient looking black pitcher silhouetted in a cloudy, gray-blue field if not an apparition lost in time, searching for a resting place?

We seek affinities not because of what they may tell us about the genetics or psychologies of the artists before us, but because of what they reveal about art itself as it has been pursued by these three vigorous visionaries. Kandinsky might call what we're after "inner meaning," the impulse that drives every artist to create certain "forms." Happily, in this pursuit we are supported by the post-Duchamp dictum that it is the viewer who completes the work of art. We are thus free to speculate on a variety of meanings, for no work of art is suffocated by one meaning only. In the case of these

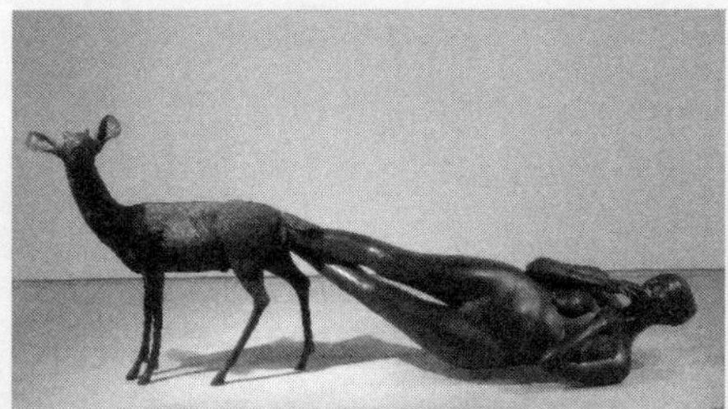

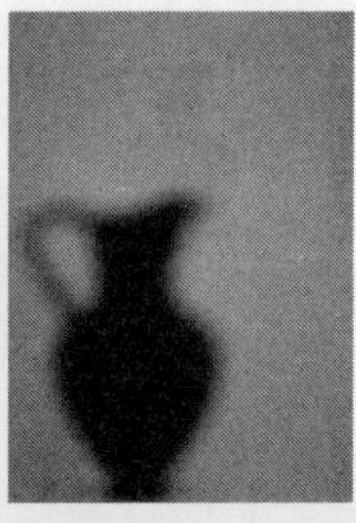

LEFT, KIKI SMITH
BORN, 2002
RIGHT, SETON SMITH
HEART PITCHER (FROM *ANNEXED THINGS*), 1997

three extraordinary artists, multiple meanings are invited and, one hopes, accepted, at least by Seton and Kiki who are still in a position to call our bluff. Tony, alas, must suffer in silence the thoughts and theories tossed about by critics, curators and historians.

In an interview in *Artforum* in 1966 Tony Smith said, "I'm just aware of basic form."[2] Spoken in true minimalist fashion, he meant that he was not concerned with the "effects," as he called them, of sculptural forms. What mattered was form itself, not an aesthetic of form. He also said he "never thought of (his work) as sculptures. I thought of them as basic design."[3] That the world came to appreciate him as "artist" was another issue he rejected. "I've never felt like an artist—it's a conduit for spiritual things—I've never felt in command of artistic media."[4]

100/101 In this barrage of what now seem to us like contradictions (a *non-artist* created the gloriously complex bronze, *Fermi*, 1973, or the burnt-red and black abstraction on canvas, *Untitled*, 1962-63?) Smith was actually echoing what many artists of stature have long engaged in: attraction to opposites and a dialectic of denial. It was a favorite game of the minimalists and conceptualists to deny the beauty in their work; to undermine the poetic in favor of the reductive. In fact, as we seek the "spiritual"[5] in Tony's work, we find an art of opposites, an art of tension and gravity that bespeaks a lightness, not a heaviness.

Certainly there is an intentional, humorous lightness in many works from *Cigarette*, 1961, and *Gracehoper*, 1962, to *She Who Must be Obeyed*, 1971-72, but the lightness I mean is similar to that expressed by Italo Calvino in one of his *Six Memos for the Next Millenium*.[6] For Calvino lightness, and not solidity, is what defines the world. He

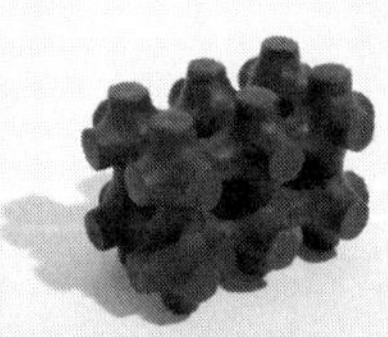

TONY SMITH, *FERMI*, 1973

refers to the poet Lucretius who believed that emptiness is just as concrete as solidity, for "matter is made up of invisible bodies."[7] This invisibility infers a profound lightness.

Of his enormous sculptures, Tony Smith said, "I don't think of them as objects, but as seeds or germs."[8] In other words, he saw them as tiny elements, like atoms, whose largeness is not measured in size but in potential and meaning. Surely, we are in the land of poetry, if not dreams, if we are to believe that a 24 x 48 x 34 foot sculpture (*Smoke*, 1967-68) is but a seed. For the artist, despite other protestations about the centrality of form, what ultimately was meaningful to him, "was the inscrutability and the mysteriousness of the thing. Something obvious on the face of it…is of no further interest."[9]

Spend time with the fleeting images of Seton Smith, images that seem to be erasing themselves before our eyes, and the straight-on, documentary flavor of so much contemporary photography (Thomas Struth, Rineke Dijkstra, Catherine Opie) can appear harsh, burdened by too much truth. Seton's entire enterprise might be described as the attempt to capture spirit as it passes among us.

She shares with her father a preoccupation with space, but for her, space is not inhabited (again: opposites, contradictions). It is rather the locus of time spent, time past, not to be recaptured. This is why her photographs seem to recede. She uses soft focus because the "real" moment has already passed. What we are seeing are the remnants, the fragments of time left behind. The "luminous light," to borrow from Roland Barthes, that suffuses her photographs does not produce clarity. It tends to blind, or at least to obscure the image as if it were our eyes that were old rather than

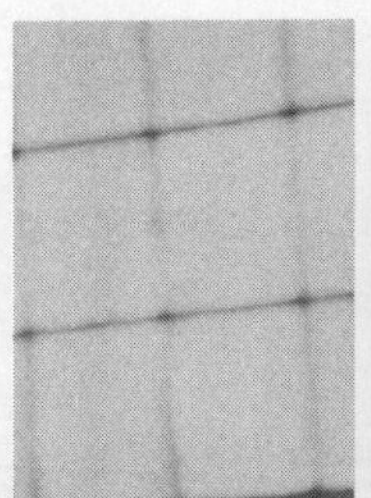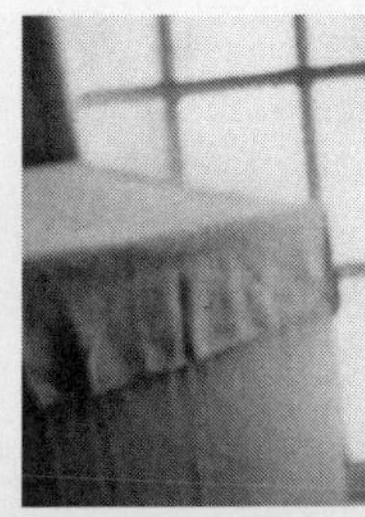

SETON SMITH
WINDOW & BED (FROM *WINDOWS FROM A CLEAR*), 1997

the objects we struggle to see. The diptych *Window & Bed*, 1997, for example, is not only out of focus, like most of our memories, but the objects pictured, as if through a glass, darkly, are also on edge, tilted. Their natural grids and straight angles have been subverted by Seton's off-kilter composition. We need to close our eyes to feel comfortable with the images, for this is the posture of sleep where dreams live.

Kiki Smith's intimate explorations of the body might seem at odds with any suggestion of a familial affinity for dreams and spirituality. In works like *Glass Stomach*, 1985, *Uro-Genital System (Female)* and *(Male),* both 1986, *Digestive System*, 1988, *Ribcage*, 1987, and *Cross-section of the Head*, 1989, to name but a few, the work was as titled. It was rather matter-of-fact, like a sculpture-cum-anatomy lesson by a craftsperson who was interested in the minimal components of human, physical life.

If we speak of dreams we must also allow for nightmares. Kiki told an interviewer in 1997 "I had an image of myself as someone dead or stillborn….My father had been ill my entire childhood and he was very involved in death."[10] The fragmented body parts in Kiki's early work serve both as protests and attempts at reconciliation. They were made at the peak of the AIDS crisis when many people she knew on the Lower East Side were ravaged by disease. Her work proclaimed the body, de-mystified the body, enlivened the body and mourned the body. She made jars with fluids in them; breasts with milk flowing from them; penises with sperm running out of them. However, unlike Walt Whitman, the poet of the body, her work was not ecstatic but rather elegiac. "I feel I'm actually making physical manifestations of psychic and spiritual dilemmas," she has said. "Spiritual dilemmas are being played out physically."[11]

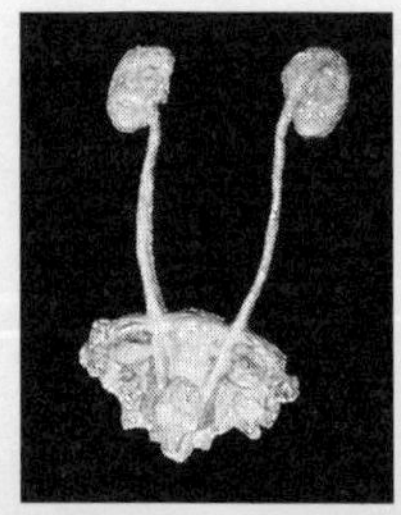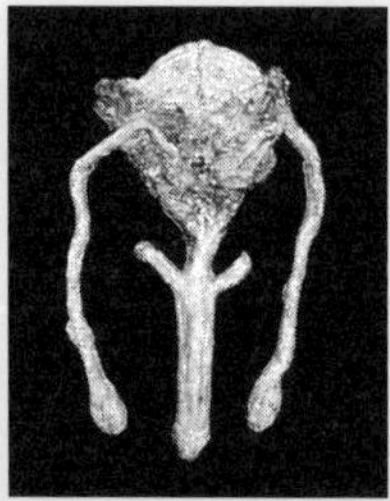

KIKI SMITH
LEFT, URO-GENITAL SYSTEM (FEMALE), 1986
RIGHT, URO-GENITAL SYSTEM (MALE), 1986

Kiki describes the trajectory of her own work this way: "I went from the microscopic to organs to systems to skins to bodies to the religious body to cosmologies."[12] In fact, she is in the process of creating her own cosmology from a wealth of materials that her sure hand knows how to manipulate. In her world, mythic beings are born anew (the spinning *Lilith*, and the upside-down blue-eyed *Lilith*, both 1994) and imagined beings come to life for the first time (*Born*, 2002); birds spring from disembodied heads (*Getting the Bird Out*, 1992) and branches of roses grow from a naked woman's back (*Untitled (Roses)*, 1993-94). The stuff of dreams? Surely. Kandinsky's inner, mystical need that calls out for expression? Absolutely.

Tony Smith thought "it was impossible to say where the boundaries of art and nature lie."[13] Perhaps if he could look into the misty light of Seton's photographs or the translucent fragility of Kiki's waxen bodies he'd see that boundary dissolving, slowly, determinedly.

Michael Rush is Director of Palm Beach ICA and an author.

1 Quoted in Hayden Herrera, *Time* magazine, October 13, 1967, reprinted in *Tony Smith*, catalogue of the exhibition, Institut Valencia D'Art Modern, 2002. 2 Samuel Wagstaff, *Talking with Tony Smith*, Artforum 5, no. 4, December, 1966, pp. 14-19. 3 Heyden Herrera, *op cit*. 4 Joan Pachner, *Writings, Interviews and Letters*, in *Tony Smith*, catalogue of the exhibition, Museum of Modern Art, New York, 1998, p. 188 5 I am using the word "spiritual" in Kandinsky's sense: the internal truth that an artist seeks to express, the boundaries of which should not be too definite. (Wassily Kandinsky, *Concerning the Spiritual in Art*, M.T.H. Sadler, trans., New York: Dover Publications, 1977, p. 9) "Spirituality," in this sense, is not to be confused with organized religion which, for Kandinsky, was one of the "lower segments of the spiritual revolution." (*Ibid.*, p. 10) 6 Calvino, Italo, *Lightness*, in *Six Memos for the Next Millenium*, Cambridge: Harvard University Press, 1988, pp. 3-30. In this essay, Calvino also enlists the novelist Milan Kundera in whose novel *The Incredible Lightness of Being* the weight of daily life moves toward lightness as individual passions and stabs at meaning rise in defiance of ubiquitous governmental oppression. 7 Ibid., p. 8. 8 Pachner, op cit, p. 190. 9 Ibid. 10 David Frankel, Interview with Kiki Smith, in Helaine Posner, *Kiki Smith*, New York: Bulfinch Press, 1998, p. 32. 11 Ibid. 12 Ibid., p. 35. 13 Pachner, op cit, p. 190.

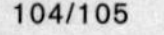

Tony Smith

Born in 1912, South Orange, New Jersey

Died in 1980, New York, New York

Selected Solo Exhibitions

1966

· *Tony Smith: Two Exhibitions of Sculpture*, Wadsworth Atheneum, Hartford, CT and Institute of Contemporary Art, Philadelphia, PA

1967

· *Tony Smith*, Bryant Park, New York, NY
· *Large Scale Sculpture by Tony Smith*, Walker Art Center, Minneapolis, MN
· *Tony Smith: The Wandering Rocks*, Galerie Müller, Stuttgart, Germany

1968

· *Tony Smith*, The Museum of Modern Art, New York, NY. A circulating exhibition, not on view at The Museum of Modern Art. Traveled to 1 Canadian and 6 United States venues.

1969

· *Sculpture by Tony Smith*, Honolulu Academy of Arts, Honolulu, HI

1970

· *9 Sculptures by Tony Smith*, Newark Museum and the New Jersey State Council on the Arts, Newark, NJ. Traveled to 6 New Jersey venues.

1971

· *Tony Smith/81 More*, The Museum of Modern Art, New York, NY

1974

· *Tony Smith: Painting and Sculpture*, University of Maryland Art Gallery, College Park, MD

1976

· *Tony Smith: Castings of Models and Small Pieces*, Fourcade, Droll Inc., New York, NY

1979

· *Tony Smith: Ten Elements and Throwback*, The Pace Gallery, New York, NY

1983

· *Tony Smith: Paintings and Sculpture*, The Pace Gallery, New York, NY

1985

· *Tony Smith Selected Sculptures: 1961-1973, Part I*, Xavier Fourcade, Inc., New York, NY; Paula Cooper Gallery, New York, NY; Margo Leavin Gallery, Los Angeles, CA

1986

· *Beyond Formalism: Three Sculptors of the 1960s: Tony Smith, George Sugarman, Anne Truitt*, The Hunter College Art Gallery, New York, NY

1987

· *Tony Smith: The Shape of Space*, List Visual Arts Center, Massachusetts Institute of Technology, Cambridge, MA
· *Tony Smith: Maze*, Paula Cooper Gallery, New York, NY

1988

· *Tony Smith: Sculptures and Drawings, 1961-1969*, Westfälisches Landesmuseum, Münster, Germany
· *Smug*, St. John's Rotary, New York, NY

1989

· *The Tony Smith Retrospective*, Jones Hall Gallery, University of St. Thomas, Houston, TX

1991

· *Tony Smith: Ten Elements*, Paula Cooper Gallery, New York, NY

1992

· *Tony Smith*, Paula Cooper Gallery, New York, NY; Galeria Theo, Madrid, Spain; and Galerie Pierre Huber, Geneva, Switzerland. A circulating exhibition, not on view at the organizing galleries. Traveled to 7 European venues.
· *Tony Smith: Paintings and Sculpture 1956-62*, Paula Cooper Gallery, New York, NY

1993

· *Tony Smith: Willy*, Paula Cooper Gallery, New York, NY

1995

· *Tony Smith, A Drawing Retrospective*, Matthew Marks Gallery, New York, NY

1997

· *Tony Smith: Moondog*, Paula Cooper Gallery, New York, NY

1998

· *Tony Smith: Architect, Painter, Sculptor*, The Museum of Modern Art, New York, NY

1999

· *Tony Smith: Stinger*, Paula Cooper Gallery, New York, NY

2001

· *Tony Smith: Painting and Sculpture 1960-1965*, Mitchell-Innes & Nash, New York, NY

2002

· *Tony Smith For Series*, Matthew Marks Gallery, New York, NY
· *Tony Smith*, Institute Valencia D'Art Modern (IVAM), Valencia, Spain

Selected Group Exhibitions

1964

· *Black, White and Gray*, Wadsworth Atheneum, Hartford, CT

1966

· *Primary Structures*, The Jewish Museum, New York, NY
· *Annual Exhibition 1966: Sculpture and Prints*, Whitney Museum of American Art, New York, NY

1967

· *American Sculpture of the Sixties*, Los Angeles County Museum of Art, Los Angeles, CA.
· *Scale As Content*, Corcoran Gallery of Art, Washington, D.C.
· *Sculpture from Twenty Nations: 5th Guggenheim International Exhibition*, The Solomon R. Guggenheim Museum, New York, NY
· *1967 Pittsburgh International Exhibition of Contemporary Painting and Sculpture*. Museum of Art, Carnegie Institute, Pittsburgh, PA

1968

· *Minimal Art*, Gemeentemuseum, The Hague, The Netherlands
· *XXXIV Biennale, Linea della Ricera: dall'informale alla nuovo strutture* (central pavillion), Venice, Italy
· *Documenta 4*, Kassel, Germany
· *The Art of the Real USA 1948-1968*, The Museum of Modern Art, New York, NY

1969

· *Minimal Art*, Akademie der Kunst, Berlin, Germany
· *New York Painting and Sculpture, 1940-1970*, The Metropolitan Museum of Art, New York, NY

1970

· *Unitary Forms: Minimal Sculpture by Carl Andre, Donald Judd, John McCracken, Tony Smith*, San Francisco Museum of Modern Art,

San Francisco, CA
· *1970 Annual Exhibition: Contemporary American Sculpture,* Whitney Museum of American Art, New York, NY

1972
· *Whitney Museum of American Art Annual,* Whitney Museum of American Art, New York, NY

1973
· *1973 Biennial Exhibition: Contemporary American Art,* Whitney Museum of American Art, New York, NY

1975
· *Sculpture: American Directions, 1945-1975,* National Collection of Fine Arts, Smithsonian Institute, Washington, D.C.

1976
· *Two Hundred Years of American Sculpture,* Whitney Museum of American Art, New York, NY

1977
· *Project: New Urban Monuments,* Akron Art Institute, Akron, OH. Traveled to 5 United States venues.

1980
· *Twenty American Artists,* San Francisco Museum of Modern Art, San Francisco, CA

1982
· *Memorial Exhibition,* American Academy and Institute of Arts and Letters, New York, NY

1984
· *BLAM! The Explosion of Pop, Minimalism, and Performance, 1958-1964,* Whitney Museum of American Art, New York, NY

1986
· *Qu'est-ce Que la Sculpture Moderne?,* Centre George Pompidou, Musée National d'Art Moderne, Paris, France
· *The Spiritual in Art: Abstract Painting 1890-1985,* Los Angeles County Museum of Art, Los Angeles, CA. Traveled to 1 European and 1 United States venue.

1987
· *Long Island Modern: The First Generation of Modernist Architecture on Long Island,* Guild Hall Museum, East Hampton, NY
· *A Century of Modern Sculpture: The Patsy and Raymond Nasher Collection,* Dallas Museum of Art, Dallas, TX. Traveled to 1 United States and 3 European venues.

1995
· *Environmental Sculptures,* Kukje Gallery, Seoul, Korea

1996
· *Abstraction in the Twentieth Century: Total Risk, Freedom, Discipline,* The Solomon R. Guggenheim Museum, New York, NY
· *Abstraction: Pure and Impure,* The Museum of Modern Art, New York, NY

1998
· *Elements of the Natural,* The Museum of Modern Art, New York, NY

2000
· *Open Ends: Minimalism and After,* The Museum of Modern Art, New York, NY

2001
· *Abstraction: the Amerindian Paradigm,* Palais des Beaux-Arts de Bruxelles, Belgium

Selected Publications

1966
· *Tony Smith: Two Exhibitions of Sculpture.* Hartford, CT: Wadsworth Atheneum, and Philadelphia, PA: Institute of Contemporary Art. Text by Samuel Wagstaff, Jr.

1968
· Battock, Gregory, ed. *Minimal Art: A Critical Anthology.* New York: E.P. Dutton, 1968. Reprinted, with an introduction by Anne M. Wagner. Berkeley and Los Angeles: University of California Press, 1995.

1970
· *Unitary Forms: Minimal Sculpture by Carl Andre, Donald Judd, John McCracken, Tony Smith.* San Francisco: San Francisco Museum of Modern Art. Text by Suzanne Foley.

1971
· *Tony Smith: Recent Sculpture.* New York: M. Knoedler & Company. Text by Martin Friedman and an interview by Lucy R. Lippard.

1972
· Lippard, Lucy R. *Tony Smith.* New York: Harry N. Abrams, Inc. and Stuttgart: Verlag Gerd Hatje.

1977
· *Project: New Urban Monuments.* Akron: Akron Art Institute. Introduction by Robert Doty and a statement by Smith.

1995
· *Tony Smith: A Drawing Retrospective.* New York: Matthew Marks Gallery. Texts by Klaus Kertess and Joan Pachner.

1998
· *Tony Smith: Architect, Painter, Sculptor.* New York: The Museum of Modern Art. Texts by Robert Storr, John Keenen and Joan Pachner.

2001
· *Tony Smith: Paintings and Sculpture 1960-65.* New York: Mitchell-Innes & Nash and Matthew Marks Gallery. Introduction by Richard Tuttle.

2002
· *Tony Smith,* Valencia Spain: Institute Valencia D'Art Modern (IVAM).

Kiki Smith

Born in 1954, Nuremberg, Germany

Lives and works in New York, New York

Selected Solo Exhibitions

1982
· *Life Wants to Live,* The Kitchen, New York, NY

1988
· Fawbush Gallery, New York, NY

1989
· *Concentrations 20,* Dallas Museum of Art, Dallas, TX

1990
· Centre d'Arte Contemporaine, Geneva, Switzerland
· Institute for Art and Urban Resources at the Clocktower, Long Island City, NY
· Institute of Contemporary Art, Amsterdam, the Netherlands
· *Projects 24: Kiki Smith,* The Museum of Modern Art, New York, NY

1991
· University Art Museum, Berkeley, CA
· Corcoran Gallery of Art, Washington, D.C.

1992
· *Unfolding the Body,* Rose Art Museum, Brandeis University, Waltham, MA
· Moderna Museet, Stockholm, Sweden
· Williams College Museum of Art, Williamstown, MA

1993
· Fawbush Gallery, New York, NY

· Phoenix Art Museum, Phoenix, AZ
· Anthony d'Offay Gallery, London, UK

1994
· University Art Museum, Santa Barbara, CA
· Louisiana Museum of Modern Art, Humlebaek, Denmark
· The Israel Museum, Jerusalem, Israel
· *Drawings,* PaceWildenstein, New York, NY
· *Kiki Smith,* Royal LePage Gallery, The Power Plant, Toronto, Canada

1995
· Whitechapel Art Gallery, London, UK
· *Sculpture & Drawings,* Anthony d'Offay Gallery, London, UK
· *New Sculpture,* PaceWildenstein, New York, NY

1996
· *Works 1988-1995,* St. Petri-Kuratorium, Lübeck, Germany
· *Field Operation,* PaceWildenstein, Los Angeles, CA
· *Kiki Smith,* Montréal Museum of Fine Arts, Montréal, Canada
· *Paradise Cage: Kiki Smith and Coop Himmelblau,* Museum of Contemporary Art, Los Angeles, CA

1997
· *Once I Saw a Bird,* Anthony d'Offay Gallery, London, UK

· *Kiki Smith: Reconstructing the Moon,* PaceWildenstein, New York, NY
· *Kiki Smith: Convergence,* Irish Museum of Modern Art, Dublin, Ireland

1998
· *Directions – Kiki Smith: Night,* Hirshhorn Museum and Sculpture Garden, Smithsonian Institution, Washington, D.C.
· *Kiki Smith,* Mattress Factory, Pittsburgh, PA
· *Invention/Intervention: Kiki Smith and the Museums,* Carnegie Museum of Art, Pittsburgh, PA
· *Kiki Smith: All Creatures Great and Small,* Kestner Gesellschaft, Hannover, Germany

1999
· *Kiki Smith: Creation,* Diözesanmuseum, Freising, Germany
· *Kiki Smith: "You Art the Sunshine Of My Life...,"* The Fruitmarket Gallery, Edinburgh, Scotland
· *Kiki Smith: Of Her Nature,* PaceWildenstein, New York, NY

2000
· *Kiki Smith,* Nassau County Museum of Art, Roslyn Harbor, NY

2001
· *Kiki Smith: Telling Tales,* International Center of Photography, New York, NY

· *Kiki Smith: Small Sculptures and Large Drawings,* Ulmer Museum, Ulm, Germany
· *Kiki Smith,* University of Wyoming Art Museum, Laramie, WY

2002
· *Kiki Smith: Realms,* PaceWildenstein and Triple Candie, New York, NY
· *Kiki Smith,* Galerie Fortlaan 17, Gent, Belgium

Selected Group Exhibitions

1980
· *Times Square Show,* New York, NY
· *A More Store,* COLAB, New York, NY

1981
· *Cave Created Chaos,* White Columns, New York, NY
· *New York, New Wave,* Institute for Art and Urban Resources at P.S.1, Long Island City, NY

1983
· *Science and Prophesy,* White Columns, New York, NY
· *Island of Negative Utopia,* The Kitchen, New York, NY

1984
· *Modern Masks,* Whitney Museum of American Art, New York, NY
· *Kiki Smith, Bill Taggert, and Tod Wizon,* Jack Tilton Gallery, New York, NY

1986
· *Public and Private: American Prints Today,* The Brooklyn Museum of Art, Brooklyn, NY
· *Momento Mori,* Centro Cultural Arte, Polanco, Mexico

1988
· *Committed to Print,* The Museum of Modern Art, New York, NY

1989
· *Projects and Portfolios,* The Brooklyn Museum of Art, Brooklyn, NY

1990
· The Renaissance Society, University of Chicago, Chicago, IL
· *Figuring the Body,* Museum of Fine Arts, Boston, MA
· *Group Material: AIDS Timeline,* Wadsworth Atheneum, Hartford, CT
· *The Unique Print: 70s into 90s,* Museum of Fine Arts, Boston, MA

1991
· *Body, Legs, Heads...and Special Parts,* Westfälischer Kunstverein, Munster, Germany
· *The Interrupted Life,* New Museum of Contemporary Art, New York, NY
· *Body Language,* Lannan Foundation, Los Angeles, CA
· *Whitney Biennial,* Whitney Museum of American Art, New York, NY
· *Burning in Hell,* Franklin Furnace, New York, NY

1992
- *Strange Behavior*, Anthony d'Offay Gallery, London, UK
- *Corporal Politics*, MIT, List Visual Art Center, Cambridge, MA
- *The Body Electric*, The Corcoran Gallery of Art, Washington, D.C.
- *Signs of Life: Rebecca Howland, Cara Perlman, Christy Rupp, and Kiki Smith*, Illinois State University Gallery, Normal, IL

1993
- *Aperto 1993*, Venice Biennale, Venice, Italy
- *Whitney Biennial*, Whitney Museum of American Art, New York, NY
- *PROSPECT 93*, Frankfurt Kunstverein, Frankfurt, Germany
- *I Am The Enunciator*, Thread Waxing Space, New York, NY

1994
- *In The Lineage of Eva Hesse*, The Aldrich Museum of Contemporary Art, Ridgefield, CT
- *World Mortality*, Kunsthalle Basel, Switzerland
- *Some Went Mad...Some Ran Away*, Serpentine Gallery, London, UK
- *Selected Works and Projects (Part One)*, Irish Museum of Modern Art, Dublin, Ireland
- *Cocido y Crudo*, Museo Nacional Centro de Arte Reina Sofia, Barcelona, Spain

1995
- *Division of Labor*, The Bronx Museum of the Arts, Bronx, NY
- *In The Flesh*, Aldrich Museum of Contemporary Art, Ridgefield, CT
- *The Material Imagination*, Guggenheim Museum SoHo, New York, NY
- *Being Human*, Museum of Fine Arts, Boston, MA
- *Feminin-Masculin: le sexe de l'art*, Musée National d'Art Moderne Centre Georges Pompidou, Paris, France

1996
- *Conceal - Reveal*, SITE Santa Fe, Santa Fe, NM
- *Everything that's interesting is new: The Dakis Joannou Collection*, DESTE Foundation, Athens, Greece

1997
- *Objects of Desire: The Modern Still Life*, The Museum of Modern Art, New York, NY
- *The Quick and the Dead: Artists and Anatomy*, Royal College of Art, London, UK

1998
- *Then and Now: Art Since 1945 at Yale*, Yale University Art Gallery, New Haven, CT
- *House of Wax*, The Contemporary Arts Center, Cincinnati, OH
- *Beyond Belief: Modern Art and the Religious Imagination*, National Gallery of Victoria, Melbourne, Australia

- *Giacometti to Judd: Prints by Sculptors*, The Museum of Modern Art, New York, NY
- *Mirror Images: Women, Surrealism and Self-Representation*, MIT List Visual Arts Center, Cambridge, MA

1999
- *As Above, So Below: The Body at Work*, The Fabric Workshop and Museum, Philadelphia, PA
- *Cosmos*, The Montréal Museum of Fine Arts, Montréal, Canada
- *The American Century: Art & Culture 1950 - 2000*, Whitney Museum of American Art, New York, NY
- *Regarding Beauty: A View of the Late 20th Century*, Hirshhorn Museum and Sculpture Garden, Smithsonian Institution, Washington, D.C.

2000
- *Unnatural Science*, Massachusetts Museum of Contemporary Art, North Adams, MA
- *End Papers: Drawings from 1890-1900 and 1990-2000*, Neuberger Museum of Art, Purchase, NY

2001
- *Heart of Glass*, Queens Museum of Art, Flushing Meadows, New York, NY
- *Digital Printmaking Now*, Brooklyn Museum of Art, Brooklyn, NY
- *God is in the Details*, Centre d'Art Contemporain, Geneva, Switzerland

2002
- *Whitney Biennial 2002 in Central Park*, Whitney Museum of American Art, New York, NY
- *La Biennale de Montréal 2002*, Cité Multimédia, Montreal, Canada

Selected Publications

1990
- *Kiki Smith*. The Hague: Institute of Contemporary Art, Amsterdam and SDU Publishers. Texts by Paolo Colombo, Elizabeth Janus, Eduardo Lipshutz-Villa, and Kiki Smith. Interview with Kiki Smith by Robin Winters.

1991
- *The Body Electric: Zizi Raymond and Kiki Smith*. Washington, D.C.: Corcoran Gallery of Art.

1992
- *Corporal Politics*. Cambridge: MIT List Visual Arts Center. Text by Helaine Posner.

1993
- *The Elusive Object*. New York: Whitney Museum of American Art. Essay by Pamela Gruninger Perkins, "Kiki Smith."

1998
- Kimmelman, Michael. *Portraits: Talking with Artists at the Met, The Modern, The Louvre and Elsewhere*. New York: Random House.
- *Kiki Smith*. New York: Bulfinch Press. Essay by Helaine Posner. Interview with the artist by David Frankel.

1999
- *The American Century: Art & Culture 1950 - 2000*. New York: Whitney Museum of American Art. Text by Lisa Phillips.
- *Regarding Beauty: A View of the Late Twentieth Century*. Washington, D.C.: Hirshhorn Museum and Sculpture Garden, Smithsonian Institution. Text by Neal Benezra and Olga M. Viso. Essay by Arthur C. Danto.

Seton Smith

Born in 1955, Newark, New Jersey

Lives and works in Paris, France

Selected Solo Exhibitions

1988
· Galerie Jule Kewenig, Frechem-Bachem, Colonia, Germany
· Tom Cugliani Gallery, New York, NY

1989
· Tom Cugliani Gallery, New York, NY

1990
· Galerie Urbi et Orbi, Paris, France

1991
· Tom Cugliani Gallery, New York, NY
· Galerie Urbi et Orbi, Paris, France
· Galerie Jule Kewenig, Frechen-Bachem, Colonia, Germany

1992
· *Parking Buirette*, Campagne Parc Auto, Reims, France
· *Northern Adventures*, St. Pancreas and Camden Arts Center, London, UK

1993
· Galerie du Dourven, O.D.D.C.-FRAC, Bretagne, France
· Galerie Urbi et Orbi, Paris, France

1994
· Musée des Beaux Arts, Nantes, France
· Centre International D' Art et de Sculpture, Crestet, France
· CRG Inc., New York, NY
· Paul Kasmin Gallery, New York, NY
· *Art Grandeur Nature*, Le Parc de la Courneuve, Paris, France
· *A Vista to Another Labyrinth Folds Back on World*, Opera Comique, Paris, France

1995
· Le Capitou, Frejus, France
· Barbara Krakow Gallery, Boston, MA
· Shoshana Wayne, Santa Monica, CA

1996
· John Weber Gallery, New York, NY
· Fotogallery, Cardiff, Wales, UK

1997
· Grand Arts, Kansas City, MO

1998
· John Weber Gallery, New York, NY
· Whitney Museum of American Art, New York, NY
· International Center of Photography, New York, NY

2001
· Cent 8, Paris, France
· Winston Wächter Mayer Fine Art, New York, NY

Selected Group Exhibitions

1979
· *Photographers*, Museum of Art and Science, Morristown, NJ

1980
· *Times Square Show*, New York, NY

1981
· Artists Space, New York, NY
· *The Positive Show* and *Island & Oasis Show*, ABC No Rio, New York, NY
· *Collaborative Projects*, Brooke Alexander, New York, NY

1982
· *Collaborative Projects*, Hallwalls, Buffalo, NY
· *A. Moore Store*, Barbara Gladstone, New York, NY

1983
· *Island of Negative Utopia*, The Kitchen, New York, NY

1985
· Group Show, Art Palace, New York, NY

1986
· *Saulen*, Galerie Jule Kewenig, Frachen-Bachem, Colonia, Germany

1988
· *Atelier '88*, Musée d'Art Moderne de la Ville de Paris, France
· *Pyramiden*, ICC, Berlin, Germany
· *Jeune Sculpture '88*, Paris, France

1989
· VIIeme Biennale Internationale de Sculpture, Skironio Museum, Athens, Greece

1991
· *L' invention du Paysage*, F.R.A.C., Corse, France

1992
· *Vers une Attitude Photographique*, Caisse des Depots et Consignations, Paris, France

1993
· *Body Count*, White Columns, New York, NY
· *The Return of the Cadavre Exquis*, The Drawing Center, New York, NY

1994
· *Sense of Place*, Elizabeth Leach Gallery, Portland, OR
· *Inspired by Nature*, Neuberger Museum, New York, NY

1995
· *Human/Nature*, New Museum of Contemporary Art, New York, NY
· *Vues Interieures*, F.R.A.C., Bretagne, France
· *Du Paysage Incertain, Fragments*, Centre Vassiviere en Limousin, France
· *Trois lieux Pour Trois Ages*, Enghien Les Bains, France
· *Morceaux choisis*, du Fonds National d'Art Contemporain, Magasin, Grenoble, France

1996
· *Reperage*, Institute of French Architecture, Paris, France
· *Photoworks/Artworks*,

John Weber Gallery, New York, NY
· *Printemps du Cahors*, Cahors, France
· *Printemps du Cahors*, Portalen, Copenhagen, Denmark
· *Inside*, California Center for the Arts Museum, Escondido, CA
· *Ouverture*, Chateau de Bionnay, Lacenas, France
· *Lush*, Christine Rose Gallery, New York, NY
· *A-Z*, Galerie Gabrielle Maubrie, Paris, France

1997
· *Landmarks*, John Weber Gallery, New York, NY
· *General Consensus*, Barbara Krakow, Boston, MA
· *Le Temps de la Marquise*, La Criee, Musée des Beaux Arts, Rennes, France
· *Matters of a Fine Wall*, Massachusetts College of Fine Art, Boston, MA
· *L'Oeil Alerte*, F.R.A.C., Bretagne, France

1998
· *Jardin D'Artiste: de Memoire d'Arbe*, Museum Zadkine, Paris, France
· *La Pluralite des Mondes*, Centre d'Art Contemporain, Kerguennec, France
· *La Nuit, L'Oubli*, Musée d' Art Moderne et Contemporain, Geneva, Switzerland
· *Le Donne, Le Fiction*, Centre National de la Photography, Paris, France

- *Still Life*, Marborough Graphics, New York, NY
- *Horsefield, Smith, Sturges*, Patrick de Brock, Knokke, Belgium
- *Collection Contemporaines*, Musée D'Art Moderne, Villeneuve D'Ascq, France

1999
- *Views From the Edge of the World*, Marlborough Chelsea, New York, NY
- *Changement d'Air*, Musée d'Art Modern Lille Metropole, Villeneuve d'Ascq, France
- Fondation for Photography CCF, La Criee, Rennes, France
- *La Criee, Rennes*, Galerie de L'Ecole des Beaux Arts, Nantes, France
- Centre Photographique de Normandie, Rouen, France

2000
- *Projects 2000*, Museum of Contemporary Photography, Chicago, IL
- *Fast: Five Years at Grand Arts*, Kansas City, MO
- *A Changing Summer*, Senior & Shopmaker, New York, NY

2002
- *Blurred Image*, Winston Wächter Mayer, Fine Art, New York, NY

Selected Site Specific Projects

1983
- *Ritz Show*, Washington, D.C.

1984
- Tin Pan Alley, New York, NY

1990
- *Parcours Prive*, Paris, France

1991
- *Escales*, Bretagne, France

1992
- Parking Buirette, Champagne Parc Auto, Reims, France
- *Northern Adventures*, St. Pancras Station and Camden Arts Center, London, UK

1994
- *Art Grandeur Nature 1994*, Le Parc de la Courneuve, France
- *A Vista to Another Labyrinth Folds Back on World*, Opera Comique, Paris, France

1995
- *Deux Aspects*, Theater/Casino, Enghien les Bains

1997
- *Blue Stairs*, Maison Europeenne de la Photographie, Paris, France

Selected Publications

1984
- *The Folding Image*. New Haven: Yale University Art Gallery. Text by M. Kowanecky, V. Fabbri Butera.

1988
- *Juene Sculpture 1988*. Paris: Association de la Jeune Sculpture.
- *ARC Atelier 1988*. Paris: Musée d'Art Moderne de la Ville Paris.
- *ARC 1983/1988*. Paris: Musée d'Art Moderne de la Ville Paris.

1990
- *Seton Smith*. Paris: Gallerie Urbi et Orbi. Essay by Jerome Sans.

1991
- *L' Invention du Paysage*. Corse: F.R.A.C. Text by S. Graziani, A. Pelenc, M. Lapalus.

1993
- Grout, Catherine. *Different Natures*. Paris: Lindau.

1994
- *Photographie D'une Collection*. Caisse des Depots et Consignations, Hazan.
- *La Salle Blanche, Seton Smith*. Nantes: Text by Jonas Storsve, Musée des Beaux Arts Nantes.
- Grout, Catherine. *Art Grandeur Nature 1994*. France: Le Parc de la Courneuve.

- Grout, Catherine. *A Vista to Another Labyrinth Folds back on World*. Paris: Opera Comique.

1995
- Foray, J.M., Jan Avgikos and Catherine Grout. *Seton Smith*. Milan: Le Capitou Electa.

1998
- *Seton Smith: Without Warning*, Paris, France: Actes/Fondation CCF pour la Photographie.

The Smiths: Tony, Kiki, Seton
Palm Beach Institute of Contemporary Art
December 3, 2002 – March 23, 2003

Published by the Palm Beach Institute of Contemporary Art
601 Lake Avenue, Lake Worth, FL 33460
561-582-0006
www.palmbeachica.org

Distributed by D.A.P./Distributed Art Publishers, Inc.
155 6th Ave, 2nd Floor
New York, NY 10013
212-627-1999 phone
212-627-9484 fax

Essays by Gilbert Brownstone, Adrian Dannatt,
Eleanor Heartney, David Pagel and Michael Rush

Edited by Michael Rush

Compiled by Jody Servon

Concept, design and production
COMA Amsterdam/New York, coma@aya.yale.edu

Printed by Veenman drukkers, The Netherlands

ISBN 0-9676480-6-8